AUTISMOLOGY

An Autism Dictionary

Tosha Rollins, MA, LPC, ASDCS

Host of *Autism in Action* Podcast

Autismology: An Autism Dictionary

All marketing and publishing rights guaranteed to and reserved by:

FUTURE HORIZONS INC.

(817) 277-0727
(817) 277-2270 (fax)
E-mail: info@fhautism.com
www.fhautism.com

ISBN: 9781949177961

ACKNOWLEDGMENTS

Autismology, An Autism Dictionary came about with the efforts of many individuals. Special thanks to the contributors and collaborators who helped make this resource available to families:

Tosha Rollins, LPC – Author

Claire Kraft – Research & References

Alexandra Peters – Research & References

Amy Sippl, MS, BCBA – Research & References

Rachel Knight – Research & References

Chris Hanson, Life Skills Advocate – Collaborator

Becky Large, Champion Autism Network – Collaborator

CONTENTS

CONTENTS

FOREWORD

Autismology is a much-needed resource for parents and people living with autism. Capturing key phrases in the increasingly accepted neurodiversity movement, Tosha gives readers much needed information to better navigate the complex medical systems affecting the care of themselves or loved ones. Tosha gives readers a fresh perspective on the ever-growing culture of neurodiversity. She provides readers the language of autism, a much-needed step in solidifying a movement that has been around for almost 30 years. This work is necessary for any professional working with mental health who wishes to serve people with autism. Autism Spectrum Disorder remains ever pressingly challenging to live with and this text is a much-needed edition to understanding the language of its increasingly accepted culture.

> — Sean M Inderbitzen, LCSW,
> therapist and person on
> the autism spectrum

LETTER FROM THE AUTHOR

As a young mom, I often had a very hard time understanding autism. I was very overwhelmed having two children on the autism spectrum. When they were diagnosed nearly two decades ago, there wasn't much of an explanation from medical professionals. I learned a lot on my own searching online while searching for answers and talking to supportive friends. Oftentimes I would find out something I hadn't discovered yet on accident by simply talking to others about autism. I would run across one website to another and before I knew it, I felt even more overwhelmed and frustrated that I couldn't find the answers I was looking for in one place. One resource would have some of the answers, and another website may have additional information. This sparked my interest in creating a dictionary reference for parents and professionals. This resource took over four years to create and a lot of cross-referencing online and collaboration with others to pull information together into one valuable resource. My hope is that it helps to cultivate conversations about autism and spreads autism awareness throughout your community. I also hope it serves as a guide to seek out additional resources that you may not have heard of before. I hope this culmination of definitions serves medical professionals well to help identify and inform patients about the language autism families are learning as they travel through their individual journeys in autism. Please know that these definitions are not all inclusive, as this field is ever changing and growing in knowledge. This dictionary can also serve the academic world by helping students who will become future medical professionals to implement a more inclusive, educated, and culture-aware point of view through the education of language through the lens offering an autism perspective.

ABC DATA
A system of data collection used in Applied Behavioral Therapy, referred to as ABA therapy, as well as in educational settings. ABC data is collected through direct observation and reports when problematic or disruptive behavior in the environment. ABC is an abbreviation for: Antecedent (something that occurs immediately before a behavior), Behavior (a detailed description of the action or behavior), and Consequence (something that occurs immediately after a behavior takes place). Parents and educators may be asked to record ABC data prior to an IEP evaluation. [2]

ABELISM
Ableism is a particular set of beliefs or practices that devalue or discriminate against people with certain physical, intellectual, or psychiatric disabilities and mostly assumes that disabled people need to be 'fixed.' Limiting beliefs about disabled individuals intertwined in our culture that impact certain perspectives or limited views on how able-bodied people treat individuals with disabilities. [3]

ABERRANT
Behavior that is significantly unlike or contrasts from what is normally accepted as usual in a culture or society. [4]

ABNORMAL BEHAVIOR
Behaviors that are significantly different from what is considered acceptable or normal in a culture or society. [4]

ABSTRACT THINKING
Thinking characterized by using generalized ideas, thoughts, or concepts. [5]

ACCOMMODATION
Adjustment, adaptation, revision, or modification to meet needs of individuals with disabilities. [5]

ACROSS MODALITIES
In teaching terms, this means teaching methods that can use one or several of the senses, such as visual (seeing), auditory (hearing), tactile (touch), and kinesthetic (movement). Also referred to as multi-sensory teachings. [4]

ADAPTIVE BEHAVIOR
Encompassing the ability to adjust to new experiences, interact or communicate with new people and participate in brand new activities or try new experiences. [6]

ADAPTIVE EQUIPMENT
The ability to adjust to brand new experiences, communicate with new people, and engage in new activities or experiences. [6]

ADAPTIVE (FUNCTIONAL) SKILLS
Skills used in daily lives in the home and community settings. Some examples of adaptive skills include: functional independence, self-reliance, problem-solving, decision-making, self-monitoring, coping skills, social pragmatics, social skills, social communication, and pursuit of leisure activities. [7]

ADMISSION, REVIEW, DISMISSAL (ARD)
ARD meetings are held to admit, review, or dismiss students into special education programs. This process occurs prior to an Individual Education Program, or IEP, being implemented by a school district. [8]

ADVOCACY
Actions of an individual that support a cause. Autism advocacy might involve attending events, meeting with community, meeting with stakeholders, and providing education to people who are unfamiliar with autism. [9]

ADVOCATE
Someone who helps someone else by acting or taking action on their behalf. [4]

AIDE
A one-to-one (1:1) aide is a category of paraprofessional or Educational Support Professional (ESP) who is assigned to only one student at a time. The student could need help learning social skills, transitioning between activities or locales, remaining on task, completing daily life skills, or lessening challenging behavior. [10]

AFFIRMATION
Positive self-talk or encouraging and positive thoughts, sentences, or phrases themself for the purpose of encouraging positive feelings, behavior, and confidence. [11]

ALERT PROGRAM
A program used to teach self-regulation awareness. The program helps children, teachers, parents and therapists to choose strategies that change or maintain states of alertness. [4]

ALEXITHYMIA
The lack of ability to identify emotions and their subtleties. [12]

ALLISTIC
Non-autistic individuals. Sometimes allistic may be used inter-changeably with "neurotypical"; Note: all non-autistics are allistics. [13]

ALTERNATIVE AND AUGMENTATIVE COMMUNICATION (AAC)
A device and or tool that helps people with communication disorders express themselves. These devices range from simple picture boards to computer programs or apps that synthesizes speech from text. [14]

AMERICANS WITH DISABILITIES ACT (ADA):
A law passed in 1990 initiated under federal civil rights law. The ADA prohibits discrimination based on disability in many different areas including: employment, state and local government, public accommodations, commercial facilities, transportation, telecommunications, and the US Congress. [15]

ANALYSIS OF VERBAL BEHAVIOR (AVB)
An applied behavior analysis approach used to teach commu-nication. AVB utilizes the abundant and effective procedures based on ABA (e.g., reinforcement, prompting, fading, task analysis). A key feature is the use of Skinner's (1957) analysis of the functions of language (e.g., to request, name things, refer to things not immediately present), this deviates from the devel-opmentally based language approach. The functional analysis of language is a key method for teaching communication skills to individuals with autism. [4]

ANGELMAN SYNDROME
A rare genetic disorder that causes severe learning impairment, difficulties, or deficits. Children display characteristics such

as: happy appearance (smiles and laughs a lot), hand flapping, excitable personality, balance problems, short attention span, developmental delay, and speech impairment with better receptive language skills. [4]

ANNUAL GOALS
Statements that identify knowledge, skills and/or behaviors a student can expected to be able to demonstrate within an academic year during which the IEP is implemented. [16]

ANTECEDENT, BEHAVIOR, CONSEQUENCE (ABC) DATA SHEET
An ABC data sheet is an assessment tool used to collect data that should evolve into a behavior implementation plan. ABC stands for: *Antecedent*: the events, action, or circumstances that occur before a behavior. *Behavior*: The behavior. *Consequences*: The action or response that follows the behavior. [2]

ANTICONVULSANT: PHARMACEUTICAL
Medications used to regulate seizures. [6]

ANTIPSYCHOTIC DRUGS
Medications that help counteract or reverse psychosis. Psychosis relates to a loss of contact with reality from a psychological perspective. [4]

ANXIETY
Anxiety is a common co-morbid diagnosis associated with individuals with autism spectrum disorder (ASD). The DSM-5 refers to this as Generalized Anxiety Disorder. Approximately 40% of presenting cases with ASD are diagnosed with comorbid anxiety disorders. Anxiety disorders include disorders that share features of excessive fear and anxiety and related

behavioral disturbances. Fear is the emotional response to a real or perceived imminent threat, whereas anxiety is the anticipation of a future threat. These two states may overlap, but they also differ. Fear is more often associated with surges of autonomic arousal necessary for fight or flight, thoughts of immediate danger, and escape behaviors. Anxiety is more often associated with muscle tension and vigilance in preparation for future threats and cautious or avoidant behaviors. Sometimes the level of fear or anxiety is reduced by pervasive avoidance behaviors. [17] [18] [19]

APHASIA
A disorder caused by damage to areas of the brain that are responsible for language. The disorder impedes the expression and or understanding of language, along with reading and writing. Aphasia may simultaneously co-occur with speech disorders, such as dysarthria or apraxia of speech, that result from brain damage. [20]

APPLIED BEHAVIORAL ANALYSIS (ABA)
Applied Behavioral Analysis, or ABA, is an evidence-based intervention for autism. ABA therapy involves teaching alternative replacement behaviors and identifying behaviors that interfere with social interaction, communication, and independent living. ABA involves positive reinforcement and data collection to shape behavior and works to change the social consequences of existing behavior. [21]

APRAXIA
(referred to as "dyspraxia" if mild) A neurological disorder characterized by loss of an ability to carry out or execute skilled movements or gestures despite a desire and physical ability to perform them. Apraxia results from dysfunction of the brain's

cerebral hemispheres and can arise from many different diseases or brain damage. [22]

ARTICULATION
Physical movements of the tongue, lips, teeth, and jaw to cause sequences of speech sounds. The speech sounds would normally make up words and sentences. Articulation is the ability to speak or produce speech sounds. [23]

ASPERGER PROFILE
A name that was adopted or chosen by the Asperger/Autism Network (AANE) to describe certain characteristics that were formerly recognized as Asperger Syndrome (AS). AS no longer exists. The formal diagnosis was defined by the medical and psychiatric community, which has now assumed the diagnosis under the much larger "Autism Spectrum Disorder" umbrella according to the most recent 5th edition of the Diagnostic and Statistical Manual (DSM-5).

AANE has chosen the term Asperger profile to identify specific challenges and recognize strengths or gifts of those who previously would meet the criteria for AS. Because of their atypical combination of strengths and challenges, individuals with an Asperger profile are often misunderstood, and their challenges either go unrecognized, or they are not diagnosed at all or are misdiagnosed. [24]

ASPERGER SYNDROME
A diagnostic label that was formerly used to describe individuals with a developmental disorder on the Autism spectrum. Asperger Syndrome was eliminated with the publication of the 5th edition of the Diagnostic and Statistical Manual (DSM-5). All individuals who meet the diagnostic criteria receive a diagnosis of autism spectrum disorder. Asperger Syndrome was formerly

characterized by average to above-average cognitive ability, deficits in communication and social language (pragmatics), and a limited range of interests and or obsessive interests in a particular topic. Examples of these interests include the weather, train schedules, or car models. [25]

ASPIE
An affectionate name often used to describe someone person diagnosed with Asperger Syndrome. It is mostly used in a favorable admiration or spirit of affirmation. [24]

ASSESSMENT
The collection of data to evaluate an individual's behavior, abilities, and other characteristics. An assessment is mainly administered to make a formal diagnosis or medical treatment recommendation. Psychologists administer assessments to diagnose diverse psychiatric problems like anxiety, depression, or substance abuse as well as and nonpsychiatric concerns like intelligence or career interests. Assessments can range across a variety of contexts including clinical, educational, organizational, forensic, and other settings. Common ASD assessments include interviews, standardized tests, self-report measures, physiological or psychophysiological measurement devices, and other tailored procedures. [5]

ASSISTIVE AND AUGMENTATIVE COMMUNICATIONS (AAC)
Additional supplies, supports, equipment, and electronic devices that offer assistance and help individuals communicate when their spoken language is not able to meet their needs. [6]

ASSISTIVE LISTENING DEVICE (ALD)
A device that serves as a tool to amplify sounds in an individual's environment, particularly where there is an extreme amount of background noise. [26]

ASSISTIVE TECHNOLOGY (AT)
Assistive technology aids individuals with disabilities and can include mobility devices like walkers and wheelchairs, hardware and software, and peripherals that can assist individuals with disabilities in accessing computers or additional information technologies. [27]

ATTENTION DEFICIT DISORDER (ADD)
A condition referring to extreme difficulty in concentrating and focusing or excessive distractibility. [6]

ATTENTION DEFICIT HYPERACTIVITY DISORDER (ADHD)
A neurodevelopmental disorder characterized by difficulty paying attention, disorganization, and managing impulsive behaviors. Inattention and disorganization may create challenges and propose difficulty with executive functioning activities like staying on task, following directions, and misplacing materials at higher rates than in same-aged peers. Hyperactivity-impulsivity includes characteristics of over-activity, fidgeting, an inability to remain seated, intruding into other people's activities, and inability to patiently wait. [18]

ATTENTION OR ATTENTION SPAN
A mental or neurological process of concentrating on one thing meanwhile ignoring other things. [4]

ATYPICAL
Not typical or normal; not relating to the standard form, or specific type. [28]

AUDIOLOGY
A study of science that relates to hearing, balance, and related disorders. Audiology evaluations are often required when diagnosing young children with autism to rule out additional conditions which could impact language development. Audiologists administer testing for auditory processing disorder and other hearing impairments. [29]

AUDITORY INTEGRATION TRAINING (AIT)
An academic intervention geared at assisting children and adults in succeeding with social interaction and learning abilities. [30]

AUDITORY MEMORY
The skillset or ability to receive data or information presented verbally, and to engage in mental interpretation, storage, and retrieval of it. [6]

AUDITORY PROCESSING DISORDERS (APD:
A diagnosis characterized by difficulty understanding and or interpreting sound in an environment. It involves challenges with hearing auditory cues in the environment, tuning out background noise, and sequencing auditory information. [31]

AUGMENTATIVE COMMUNICATION
Methods of communication to enhance or replace standard forms of communication or spoken language. People with significant deficits in communication skills can rely on augmentative communication systems to communicate their needs, wants, thoughts, and feelings. There are many augmentative

communication systems available like gestures, sign language, picture exchange (e.g., PECS), pointing to pictures, and electronic devices that include voice output. [4]

AUTISM BEHAVIOR CHECKLIST (ABC)

Autism Behavior Checklist is a screening tool for autism spectrum disorder. The Autism Behavior Checklist (ABC) is a list of questions that requests information about a child's behaviors. The ABC Checklist screening is completed independently by a parent or teacher familiar with the child, who then returns it to a trained professional for scoring and interpretation.

The ABC has fifty-seven questions separated into five categories: (1) sensory, (2) relating, (3) body and object use, (4) language, and (5) social and self-help. [32]

AUTISM DIAGNOSTIC INTERVIEW-REVISED (ADI, ADI-R)

The Autism Diagnostic Interview–Revised (ADI–R) is an assessment used to aide in the diagnosis of autism spectrum disorders in children as well as adults. The test administrator interviews the parent or caregiver to collect detailed information related to that of past and current behaviors relevant to an autism spectrum disorder diagnosis. The assessment focuses on developmental delays, social interactions, language, nonverbal communication, play, understanding and expression of emotions, and on restricted, repetitive, and stereotypic behaviors and interests. [4]

AUTISM DIAGNOSTIC OBSERVATION SCHEDULE (ADOS)

A widely used assessment to diagnose autism. The Autism Diagnostic Observation Schedule, Second Edition (ADOS-2) is a semi-structured set of observations and series of activities involving the referred individual and a trained examiner. Trained evaluators can conduct the ADOS with individuals as young as twelve months old to verbally fluent adults. [33]

AUTISM MENTAL STATUS EXAM (AMSE)

The AMSE is an eight-item observational assessment that helps to structure the way licensed professionals observe, track, and document social, communicative, and behavioral functioning in individuals diagnosed with autism. [34]

AUTISM OBSERVATION SCALE FOR INFANTS (AOSI)

A testing instrument created in Canada that is used to measure autism-related behaviors in infants and toddlers to assess what their overall risk of later developing autism will be. [4]

AUTISM SPECTRUM DISORDER (ASD)

A developmental disorder impacting communication and social behavior. Although ASD can be diagnosed at any age, it is a "developmental disorder" because symptoms generally appear in the first two years of life. According to the *Diagnostic and Statistical Manual of Mental Disorders* (DSM-5), autism involves:

- difficulty with communication and interaction with others
- restricted interests or repetitive behaviors
- symptoms that impact a person's ability to function properly in school, work, and other life areas

Autism is a spectrum disorder because there are wide variations in the type and symptoms different individuals experience. ASD occurs in all ethnic, racial, and socio-economic groups. Although ASD can be a lifelong disorder, treatments and services can improve a person's symptoms and ability to function. The American Academy of Pediatrics recommends that all children be screened for autism. [18, 35]

AUTISTIC SAVANT
A person diagnosed with autism who excels in an exceptional skill in some limited field (e.g., music, math). [4, 36]

AVERSIVES
An aversive is a very unpleasant event or object that an individual will actively attempt to avoid. Aversive consequences are known as "punishers" when they are given as a consequence of a behavior, and this causes results to display the behavior occurring less frequently. The term punisher is a term used in behavioral therapy, and does not imply the use of physical aversives, like hitting, slapping, or spanking. Mild verbal disagreement or withholding a preferred object or activity might also serve as punishers for younger children. [4]

BABBLING
Referred to as a language development stage characterized by a child experimenting with sounds but not yet speaking recognizable words. Canonical babbling is considered a critical milestone in speech development. It is usually well developed by around ten months of age. Some research suggests that children with ASD show late developmental onset of babbling. [37]

BASELINE
An initial set of observations, data sets, or information used for control measures or comparison. Baseline data serves as a benchmark to measure progress or decline in what is being measured. [38]

BAYLEY SCALES:
An evaluation or assessment tool used to evaluate, assess, test, and diagnose developmental delays. The Bayley Scales measure child development across five different domain categories

including: Cognitive, Language (Receptive & Expressive), Motor (Gross & Fine), Social-Emotional, and Adaptive. This measure can evaluate children ages one month to forty-two months to identify individuals who may benefit from early intervention screening and services. [39]

BEHAVIOR INTERVENTION PLAN (BIP)/BEHAVIOR SUPPORT PLAN (BHS)

A written plan that aids with interfering, impairing, or disruptive problematic behaviors. The plan teaches replacement behaviors to aid in obtaining positive behavior results. Intervention or support plans are frequently developed alongside development of an Indivudualized Education Plan (IEP) or alongside additional intervention services. These types of plans traditionally have three essential parts: a definition of the problem behavior, a description of the function or why it's happening, and supportive strategies or accommodations. [40]

BEHAVIOR INTERVENTIONIST (BI)

Refers to a medical professional or other professional who works with a child to make progress towards and achieve specified goals, typically goals outlined or defined by a behavioral consultant. This person usually works directly with a child in a one on one setting. [4]

BEHAVIORAL HEALTH REHABILITATION SERVICES (BHRS)

Services tailored for individuals with a severe impairment concerning emotional, behavioral, or developmental disability. The goal of BHRS is to help an individual reduce impairment and progress with greater autonomy and independence at home, school, and in their community. [41]

BEHAVIOR MODIFICATION
The implementation of empirically based behavior change techniques aimed to decrease impairment and improve positive outcome behaviors. [6]

BERARD AUDITORY INTEGRATION TRAINING (BERARD AIT OR AIT)
Intervention where the service provider identifies or recognizes sounds to which the person is believed to be over- or under-sensitive. Music with selected high and low frequencies is presented with the use of headphones worn by the participant. Certain sounds or frequencies may be fully or partially filtered or removed from the music. In Auditory Processing Training, speech sounds are dilated or expanded (i.e., presented slower than in normal speech patterns), and then compressed while the person progresses. Some examples include: Tomatis method, Berard Method, Earobics, Fast Forward. [4]

BCBA
A Board-Certified Behavior Analyst, or an individual certified by the Behavior Analyst Certification Board in Applied Behavior Analysis. BCBAs frequently specialize in creating communication, social, and behavioral interventions for individuals with autism and other developmental delays.

BLENDED INTERVENTION
A treatment method which combines various disciplines and therapy techniques together. An example is ABA therapy that combines discrete trial intervention (DTI) with natural environment teaching (NET) techniques. Blended interventions have shown promise with individuals with autism, especially when they are individualized to teach specific skills through ways in which the learner is likely to acquire them fastest. [42]

CENTRAL AUDITORY PROCESSING DISORDER

Central Auditory Processing Disorder (CAPD) is a learning where individuals hear sounds but are unable to process or translate them correctly into words or language. Individuals diagnosed with CAPD may have difficulty understanding what they are hearing, and trouble acting on it quickly, remembering it for a short or periods of time, and creating or responding verbally. Professionals like speech-language pathologists and audiologists are usually involved in diagnosing and treating auditory processing disorders. [4]

CENTRAL COHERENCE

A descriptive term used in psychology to identify an individual's ability to translate or recall large amounts of information. Persons with well-developed central coherence can quickly contextualize or visualize the bigger picture. [24]

CENTRAL NERVOUS SYSTEM

The body's control center, comprised of the brain and spinal cord. [4]

CEREBELLUM

The lower back part of the brain that controls functions like maintaining balance, coordinating, and controlling certain voluntary muscle movements. [4]

CEREBRAL CORTEX

The outer layer of gray matter in the brain in which higher brain functions occur. Examples include sensation, voluntary movement, thought, reasoning, and memory. [4]

CHECKLIST FOR AUTISM IN TODDLERS (CHAT)

A screening instrument or tool used to detect and screen autism in younger age children. It provides the first level of screening and or evaluation, leading to a yes/no decision that currently autism is unlikely or that it is possible and likely requires further assessment. The CHAT was published in 1992 and takes approximately five to ten minutes to administer and interpret results. It can be used with children as young as eighteen months of age. [43]

CHILDHOOD AUTISM RATING SCALE (CARS)

The Childhood Autism Rating Scale (CARS) is the most widely recognized standardized instrument designed to detect and diagnose autism in children starting as young as two years old. It was originally published in 1980 and correlated to the DSM-III and then to the DSM-III-R. It is a direct observational tool used by a trained clinician and takes approximately twenty to thirty minutes to take.

It includes fifteen specific direct observational items that measure areas including: Relationships with People, Imitation, Affect, Use of Body, Relation to Non-human Objects, Adaptation to Environmental Change, Visual Responsiveness, Auditory Responsiveness, Near Receptor Responsiveness, Anxiety Reaction, Verbal Communication, Nonverbal Communication, Activity Level, Intellectual Functioning, and the clinician's overall diagnostic impression. [43]

CHILD BEHAVIOR CHECKLIST (CBCL)

The CBCL is a component of the Achenbach System of Empirically Based Assessment (ASEBA). It is used to discover behavioral and or emotional deficits or areas of impairment in children as well as adolescents. The CBCL is completed by parents. [44]

CHILDHOOD DISINTEGRATIVE DISORDER

A form of pervasive developmental disorder in which normally developing children suddenly lose language and social skills after age three. This can also be referred to as regression. It is a relatively rare diagnosis that resembles autism and occurs often in three- to four-year-olds. It is characterized by a deterioration of intellectual, social, and language functioning from prior normal observed functioning. It is considered a pervasive developmental disorder although it is not included as Autism Spectrum Disorder. Autism Spectrum Disorder has additional diagnostic criteria that must be met. [4, 6]

CHILD PSYCHOLOGIST

A licensed mental health professional who professionally administers, scores, and interprets psychological assessments, evaluates and treats specific emotional, developmental, and behavioral disorders of children and adolescents. Psychologists cannot prescribe medication. Psychologists usually have a credential of mastering their Ph.D. in Psychology. [4]

CHROMOSOME

A specific part in the cell nucleus contains genes. Humans normally have 46 chromosomes. [4]

CO-EXISTING DISORDERS (OR COMORBIDITIES)

Individuals with autism often suffer from multiple psychopathologies or cognitive impairments. Some examples include: impulse-control disorders, ADHD, Anxiety, Depression, Mood Disorders, psychoses, obsessive-compulsive disorder, seizures, and developmental delays. These are often referred to as co-morbid disorders or differential diagnosis or dual diagnosis. [4]

COGNITION
Having the ability to perceive, problem solve, recall, think, reason, and analyze information. [4, 6]

COGNITIVE
Intellectual activity including thinking, reasoning, or recalling information by memory. [45]

COGNITIVE ABILITY
A person's intellectual ability, including skillsets like knowing and understanding. [6]

COGNITIVE BEHAVIORAL THERAPY (CBT)
Psychological treatment that is empirically validated for a range of problems like depression, anxiety, substance use problems, marital problems, eating disorders, and additional severe mental illnesses. Empirically validated research suggests that CBT can lead to significant improvement in overall functioning and greater quality of life. [46]

COMMUNICATION DISORDER
A disorder that causes interference with an individual's ability to comprehend, express ideas, experiences, knowledge, information, or emotions. [4]

COMORBIDITY
Co-occurrence of one or several disorders or diagnosis in the same individual at the same time. [47]

COMPLEMENTARY AND ALTERNATIVE MEDICINE (CAM)

A group of many different types of health care systems, practices, or not considered to be part of conventional medicine. Sometimes this can be referred to as functional medicine practices. [4]

COMPREHENSIVE EVALUATION

A complete evaluation of a child that is based on specific educational, psychological, social, and health information that is administered by a team of medical professionals. Oftentimes this evaluation is complemented by data or additional input from parents and teachers. [6]

COMPULSION

An uncontrollable impulse or urge to perform a specific act, sometimes performed repetitively, and usually aimed at avoiding or alleviating anxiety. [4]

CONGENITAL OR CONGENITAL CONDITION

A condition inherent biologically since birth. [4,6]

CONSULTATION

Case discussion and assessment or evaluation focused on data, information, goals, objectives, and therapeutic techniques to be implemented. [4]

CONVULSION

Violent, disturbing, and or involuntary contractions or series of contractions of the muscles in a body. [48]

COPING SKILL

Any implemented behavioral pattern that enhances a person's daily functioning. Coping skills can include a religious belief system, problem solving, social skills, health considerations, and social support systems. [49]

COREGULATION

The process where infants and children develop an ability to soothe and manage distressing emotions and sensations birth through connection with caregivers that are nurturing and reliable. It involves different types of responses like a warm, calming presence, a calm tone of voice, verbal or facial acknowledgement of distress, modeling types of behaviors, and providing a structured environment that supports emotional and physical stability and or safety. [50]

CORTISOL

A specific steroid hormone that is produced and released by your adrenal and endocrine glands. Cortisol is responsible for several aspects of your body's healthy functioning. It also helps manage your body's response to stress. [51]

CUE

A physical, verbal, or nonverbal signal or prompt. [52]

CURRICULUM

A set of specified course objectives that lead to learning outcomes. [4]

DAILY SCHEDULE

A structured outline of specified activities or tasks for a twenty-four-hour time period. It offers predictability and helps an individual make transitions from one task to the next task. A daily schedule is useful for maximizing on task or engaged behaviors and minimizing inappropriate behaviors. This kind of schedule can be provided in various written or visual forms. [4]

DATA COLLECTION

The gathering of very specific, detailed, objective information about an individual's performance in an academic or behavioral context. Data is usually presented in a quantitative format (e.g., the number of times a behavior presents, percentage correct performing tasks, amount of work performed.). The data that is collected or analyzed helps to evaluate the effectiveness of a program. Data collection has two important parts: information gathering and decision making. Information gathering may include curriculum-based assessments, observing classroom behaviors, grading papers, or conducting parent interviews. Data based decisions might impact changes regarding curriculum, teaching styles, or the management of behaviors in an academic setting. [4]

DEVELOPMENTAL

Pertains to processes related to growth, maturation, or progressive change in an individual as they grow older. [4]

DEVELOPMENTAL DELAY

A diagnosis that occurs when a child does not reach age level developmental milestones. It can be considered an ongoing major or minor delay in the developmental process. Delays are considered those not likely to catch up without early intervention.

A delay can occur in one or several areas (i.e., gross or fine motor, language, social, or thinking skills). [53]

DEVELOPMENTAL, INDIVIDUAL DIFFERENCES, RELATIONSHIP-BASED (DIR)

An intervention framework that helps clinicians, parents and educators conduct a comprehensive evaluation and create an intervention plan that is individualized to the unique challenges and strengths of an individual. [54]

DEVELOPMENTAL DISABILITIES (DD)

Diagnostic conditions including impairments in physical, learning, language, and or behavior areas. These conditions often start during the developmental period, can impact day-to-day functioning, and usually last throughout a person's overall lifetime. [56]

DEVELOPMENTAL LANGUAGE DISORDER

Children can be diagnosed with language disorders when they experience and present with problems, not due to injury, like expressing their thoughts, understanding written material, or understanding what others say. [4]

DEVELOPMENTAL LEVEL

A method of watching or observing how children achieve developmental milestones, like crawling, walking, sitting, standing, and talking; particularly those related to their overall ability to stay engaged, express mutual pleasure and attention, to engage in complex problem solving, interact in symbolic play, and link ideas together. [4]

DEVELOPMENTAL MILESTONES
Skills related to playing, learning, speaking, acting, and movement that most children achieve by a certain age. [57]

DEVELOPMENTAL REGRESSION
A type of autism in which infants, after normal development, start to lose language and other skills. [4]

DIAGNOSIS
A disorder that is identified after an evaluation and given a name. [6]

DIAGNOSTIC OVERSHADOWING
The tendency for caregivers or clinicians to attribute new behaviors to the primary diagnosis (e.g., autism), when in fact they are due to a new condition (e.g., anxiety, depression, ADHD). [4]

DIAGNOSTIC AND STATISTICAL MANUAL (DSM-5 OR DSM-5-TR)
The official and only recognized medical system for classification of psychological and psychiatric disorders. This manual was prepared by and published by the American Psychiatric Association. [54]

DIFFERENTIAL DIAGNOSIS
A determined diagnosis that is given by assessing an individual's symptoms and has taken into account all possible alternative explanations, until the most likely cause, and or diagnosis is identified. [4]

DIMETHYLGLYCINE (DMG)
A non-protein amino acid found naturally in animal and plant cells, that has a history of being used to aide in immune system functioning. Research has been published prior on humans and laboratory animals with a correlation demonstrating how DMG has improved immune system functioning in prior studies. Individuals with autism sometimes can display symptoms of having a weak immune system. [4]

DIR/FLOORTIME
A therapeutic intervention and treatment approach that was created by Stanley Greenspan, M.D., and Serena Wieder, PhD. This method addresses and improves social, emotional, and intellectual capacities of persons with autism, rather than looking at isolated behaviors. DIR stands for Development, Individual Differences, Relationship-Based. Discrete Trial Training (DTT). It is a teaching method included in, but not considered synonymous with, behaviorally based interventions, like ABA. Specific skills are taught through continuous repetition of the following steps: presentation of task, response, and reinforcement, with prompts provided if and when needed. A subsequent pause follows each specific sequence, indicating the beginning and ending of every cycle. [6]

DISCRETE TRIAL INTERVENTION (DTI)
A structured, evidence-based ABA technique that breaks down skills into small, "discrete" parts. The trainer teaches these skills one by one in a systematic way. During this process, therapists use positive reinforcements for desired behaviors. Oftentimes DTI intervention is used to teach basic skills like labeling items, matching pairs, or sequencing. It can also be infused with other therapeutic techniques to teach more skills that are more complex. [58]

DOPAMINE

Type of neurotransmitter, oftentimes referred to as the chemical messenger. Your nervous system utilizes it to send and transfer messages among the nerve cells in the body.

Dopamine is sometimes referred to as the happy chemical, as its role in how we feel is often described as a feeling of pleasure. Dopamine plays a big part in our thinking and planning. [59]

DOWN SYNDROME

A condition in which a person is born with an extra chromosome. Typically, a baby is born with 46 chromosomes, while babies with Down syndrome have an extra copy of one of these chromosomes, chromosome 21. This extra copy impacts the development of the baby's body and brain develop, which can cause both mental and physical challenges for the baby. [60]

DUE PROCESS HEARING

A formal process with an impartial officer, administrative law judge, or panel of judges, for the purpose of evaluating a child's access to free appropriate public education. [61]

DX

Abbreviated word for diagnosis or diagnostic. [62]

DYNAMIC INDICATORS OF BASIC EARLY LITERACY SKILLS (DIBELS)

A set of procedures and measures for evaluating the acquisition of infant literacy skills. They are created to be very short (one-minute) fluency measures that regularly monitor skills for development of early literacy and early reading skillsets. [63]

DYSCALCULIA

A term referencing a pattern of difficulties characterized by problems with processing numerical data, learning arithmetic facts, and performing accurate or fluent calculations. [18]

DYSLEXIA

Refers to a pattern of learning difficulties characterized by deficits with identifying accurate or fluent word recognition, poor decoding, and poor spelling abilities. [18]

DYSPRAXIA

Trouble with movement including difficulty in four needed human skills like fine motor skills, gross motor skills, motor planning, and coordination. [64]

EAR TUBES

Tiny tubes that allow fluid to drain and are inserted in the eardrum. They are usually recommended for children who get recurring ear infections. [6]

EARLY INTENSIVE BEHAVIORAL INTERVENTION (EIBI)

Therapeutic intervention derived from the principles of Applied Behavior Analysis (ABA). EIBI targets children under the age of five with autism as well as other developmental disabilities. EIBI is usually characterized by intensive treatment (twenty to forty hours per week) and behavioral focus (using positive reinforcement and data collection). [54]

EARLY INTERVENTION SERVICES

Services and supports provided for infants and younger children diagnosed with developmental delays and disabilities. [65]

EARLY PERIODIC SCREENING DIAGNOSIS TREATMENT (EPSDT)

Health care services for children under age twenty-one enrolled in Medicaid that are considered preventative intervention. EPSDT is important to ensuring that children as well as adolescents receive needed preventive, dental, mental health, developmental, and specialty services. [66]

ECHOLALIA

Repetitions of vocal sounds, words, or phrases. May also be called "scripting" or "TV talk." Echolalia occurs at much higher rates in persons diagnosed with autism. Echolalia can appear like a person is repeating words out of context. However, echolalia can be considered meaningful communication. The person might repeat what you say as a way to further their understanding, because they don't understand the question being asked or how to best respond to a question. [67]

ECHOPRAXIA

When someone is mimicking the movements of another person. [18]

EHLERS-DANLOS SYNDROMES (EDS)

Several types of hereditary disorders of connective tissue that differ in the ways they affect the body and in their genetic implementation. The abnormal structure or function of collagen and certain allied connective tissue proteins seems to be a primary concern. [68]

ELECTROENCEPHALOGRAM (EEG)

Testing that detects abnormalities in brain waves as well as the electrical activity of a brain. EEG results may be helpful to diagnose seizure disorders or atypical brain activity that can be associated with a particular developmental or intellectual delay. [69]

ELIGIBILITY REQUIREMENTS
Qualifications a child must meet to participate in early intervention services. Qualifiers can include characteristics like age, disabilities, and developmental delays. [70]

ELOPEMENT
An individual fleeing an environmental setting, which puts them at risk of danger or harm. It's common for children diagnosed with autism spectrum disorder (ASD) to run away or wander from caregivers and or secure locations. [71]

EMOTIONAL FREEDOM TECHNIQUE (EFT) (OR PSYCHOLOGICAL ACUPRESSURE)
A systematic process of tapping one's forehead, temples, chest and wrist in order to release stress or anxiety. [11]

EMOTIONAL REGULATION
Describes how effective the outcomes of management and response to emotional experiences are demonstrated by an individual. [72]

ENGAGEMENT
A process considered to be purposeful with interaction and learning where children coo, smile, and make gestures with their partners. These interactions assist with building intimacy, joy, and creating a rhythmic interaction. [4]

ENVIRONMENTAL ENGINEERING
The process of arranging a physical environment to improve learning and behavior. The physical environment serves as stimuli that can significantly impact appropriate or inappropriate behaviors. This impact can have a positive affect to an individual's performance. [4]

EPIDEMIOLOGY
The study of how a specific disease affects a specific population (e.g., an epidemiologist might study how prevalent the disease or condition is or how this shifts over time, how it is distributed geographically or across age or social groups). [4]

EPILEPSY
A disorder of the central nervous system (neurological) where brain activity becomes abnormal. This causes seizures or time periods of abnormal behavior, sensations, and sometimes loss of consciousness or awareness. [73]

EQUINE THERAPY
Type of experiential therapy that involves a person interacting with horses and is focused heavily on the relationship building between the person and the horse. [74]

ETIOLOGY
A study of what causes a disease. [4]

EVALUATION CRITERIA
A part of the Individualized Education Plan (IEP). This provides a detailed description of how IEP results can determine the achievement of standard goals. Information is obtained by teacher observation, parent interviews, and standardized testing results. [6]

EVALUATIONS
A standardized process or empirically validated assessment used to identify a specific disorder, like autism, and recommend intervention or treatment services. [75]

EXECUTIVE FUNCTION (EF)
Particular skills and behaviors that allow for successful independence as an adult. Executive functioning skills include: organizational, planning abilities; working memory; inhibition and impulse control; self-reflection and self-monitoring; time-management, -prioritizing; understanding complex or abstract concepts; and adapting to using new strategies. [76]

EXPRESSIVE LANGUAGE
A subset of communication where expressive language refers to the ability of a child' to use language as a way to express himself. Expressive language can communicate needs, thoughts, and ideas to other people using words, phrases, or sentences. [77]

EXTENDED SCHOOL YEAR SERVICES (ESY)
Students can receive special education services through their school district for an extended period of time outside the normal school year calendar (e.g., summer or winter break). ESY services are written into individualized special education plans and/or related services (e.g., speech/language therapy, occupational therapy) that are tailored to provide a free appropriate public education (FAPE) to a student with disabilities (as mandated by IDEA — *see IDEA*). [78, 169]

EXTINCTION
The withholding of reinforcement for a behavior that has previously been reinforced so that it eliminates the behavior. The word "extinction" may also imply the reduction in frequency of occurrence of a certain behavior that results from withholding reinforcement. [4]

EYE GAZE
A pattern or orientation of the eyes. Eye gaze has a dual function in human social interaction—people can perceive information about others as well as use their gaze to signal to others. [79]

FACE BLINDNESS (PROSOPAGNOSIA/FACIAL AGNOSIA)
Not having an ability to recognize faces. [80]

FACILITATED COMMUNICATION
The use of a keyboard by a person with autism. The training begins with simple questions that have predictable answers, and then becomes more complex with lessened physical support from a facilitator. [4]

FAMILY-CENTERED/FOCUS MODEL
Family-centered services emphasize the family's identification of their needs, resources, and service requirements. Over the past several years, increased emphasis has been placed on enabling and empowering families to manage services and resources for their children with special needs. [4]

FAMILY TRAINING
Services provided to a family by a professional created to assist in understanding a child's individual needs to help the child's development progress. This may also be referred to as caregiver training, family skills training, or family coaching. [81]

FINE MOTOR
Activities and behaviors that use the small muscles in an individual's hands or wrists. Fine motor activities can include pinching, grasping, writing, cutting with scissors, and using utensils. [82]

Fine Motor Skills: Using one's hands for moving objects and performing specific activities. [6]

504 PLAN
A guide for how schools can or will support students with disabilities while removing or reducing any barriers to academic progress. A 504 Plan offers services and adapts the learning environment to allow students to learn in a least restrictive environment alongside their grade-level peers. [1]

FIXATION
An inability to release or let go of a repetitive thought. [11]

FLAT AFFECT
An autistic individual's inability to display emotion in their verbal or facial expressions. [11]

FLUENCY TRAINING
Training used in other programs to help individuals benefit from maximizing and generalizing and retention of learned language skills. Fluency techniques can result in increased accuracy and speed of performing speech tasks. [4]

FOOD SELECTIVITY
Restrictive or repetitive behaviors, patterns, and interests that involve foods and eating behaviors. Many children with ASD have difficulties with fixed interests and repetitive behaviors that impact their overall food preferences. Feeding intervention therapies can help or aid in refusal to eat foods, eating varied food textures, and challenges with biting, swallowing, or chewing. Food selectivity can be very distressing for parents or caregivers. [83]

FRAGILE X SYNDROME
Genetic condition which causes a range of developmental problems, like learning disabilities or cognitive impairment. Males are more severely impacted by this disorder than females. [84]

FREE APPROPRIATE PUBLIC EDUCATION (FAPE)
The right to a Free Appropriate Public Education (FAPE) is an educational entitlement of all students in the United States and considered to be one of the most important legal rights any child has. It is legally guaranteed by the Rehabilitation Act of 1973 and the Individuals with Disabilities Education Act. [85]

FUNCTIONAL ANALYSIS
A functional behavioral analysis begins as an assessment, and it includes the additional step of altering systematically the antecedents to and consequences of the behaviors to determine precisely which are the driving forces triggering that behavior. [4]

FUNCTIONAL ASSESSMENT
An assessment used in Applied Behavior Analysis therapy to determine the function or maintaining variables of a problem behavior. Functional assessments are normally conducted in very controlled, clinical, and/or educational settings by trained behavior analyst professionals. The results of this can be used to inform function-based interventions. [86]

FUNCTIONAL BEHAVIOR ASSESSMENT (FBA)
An evaluation using a combination of direct and indirect observations to determine the purpose or function of a behavior. FBAs are conducted in both special education and ABA therapy settings, allowing parents, teachers, and school professionals to collaborate on an appropriate behavior intervention plan.

Federal law requires an FBA whenever an individual with an IEP has a change in educational placement or a re-evaluation. [87]

FUNCTIONAL COMMUNICATION TRAINING (FCT)
A therapeutic program for individuals with autism focusing on targeting a specific problematic behavior and replacing it with a much safer or more appropriate communication response. The more appropriate communication should serve the same behavioral function as the problem response (e.g., asking for a break instead of elopement, asking for attention instead of screaming). FCT may also target vocal speech (e.g., asking for a break) but can be customized to use sign language, gestures, pictures, or speech-generating devices. [88]

FUNCTIONAL MEDICINE
A systems biology–based approach focusing on identifying and confronting the root cause of disease. [89]

FUNCTIONAL MRI
Magnetic resonant imaging (MRI) scanning where scientists can view what parts of the brain are active while a person is performing a certain task, like solving math problems in the MRI scanner. [4]

FUNCTIONAL PLAY
Playing with toys or objects based on their intended function (e.g., rolling a ball around, pushing a car on the table, pretending to feed an animal or doll). [90]

GENE

Genes are formed from DNA and are carried on chromosomes. They are responsible for specific inherited characteristics that distinguish one person from another. Each human individual has an estimated 100,000 separate genes. [4]

GENERALIZATION

Refers to the transfer of previously learned skills to new environmental settings. Generalization may occur across various settings, staff or caregivers, or even to new materials. Many individuals with autism have difficulty with generalization, and it oftentimes must be included in an intervention or therapeutic plan. [91]

GENERALIZED ANXIETY DISORDER (GAD)

A disorder that is characterized by excessive, prolonged worry and tension about something consistently over the course of six months. Worry is difficult to control. Additional symptoms include restlessness, feeling easily fatigued, difficulty concentrating, irritability, muscle tension, and sleep disturbance. These symptoms cause clinically significant impairment across a variety of settings like work, school, recreational, or home. [4, 18]

GENETIC

A term describing something that which relates to genes. [4]

GENETIC SYNDROME

A group of physical signs and/or symptoms that occur simultaneously in a person and characterize a specific genetic or chromosome abnormality. [4]

GENTLE TEACHING
A non-aversive therapy that emphasizes bonding between teacher and student. It was developed by John McGee, who believes that individuals who persistently hit, bite, kick, scratch, self-stimulate, or withdraw have not bonded with their caregivers and that academic teachers must help move behaviorally involved persons from a state of emotional distancing to one of meaningful human engagement so that they will not need to continue to express their needs through harmful, primitive responses. [4]

GESTALT
A term that refers to a unified whole that is more than just the sum of its parts. Gestalt language processing describes learning entire phrases or other language chunks as whole units, rather than learning all of the individual words within a chunk and combining them in unique and flexible ways. [4]

GESTALT LEARNERS
Many children with autism are gestalt learners of language because they tend to remember and use whole phrases as "chunks" or whole units. [4]

GESTURES
A form of communication using body parts instead of vocal speech. Gestures can allow people to communicate about feelings and thoughts through body language in addition to spoken words. [92]

GILLIAM AUTISM RATING SCALE (GARS)
A norm-referenced assessment tool designed to detect signs of Autism Spectrum Disorder in individuals between the ages of three and twenty-two. [93]

GLOBAL DELAY
A delay in development which includes cognitive, motor, and language abilities. [4]

GLUTEN-FREE/CASEIN-FREE (GF/CF) DIETS
A particular diet believed by some people to help improve the symptoms of autism. It includes elimination from the diet of gluten (a protein found in wheat and other grains) and casein (a protein found in milk). Gluten is found mainly in wheat, oats and barley; casein in milk products. Certain people on the autistic spectrum have reported that following a diet free from these things can help their concentration and prevent digestive problems. [4]

GOALS
Goals allow people to achieve and maintain focus in life by aiding them to determine what they want. They encourage motivation and constantly putting define a specific state of action. [94]

GOLD STANDARDS
A description of the highest standard at a particular time. [4]

GREENSPAN FLOORTIME APPROACH
An evidence-based intervention which focuses on play-based and child-driven activities. Research has demonstrated that it helps to strengthens basic communication and relationship abilities in children with autism and other special needs. [95]

GROSS MOTOR
Many individuals with autism have gross motor delays and may attend therapy interventions to address them. Many activities and/or behaviors involve the use of large muscles and coordination. Gross motor skills relate to the abilities like balance,

coordination, body awareness, physical strength, and reaction time. [96]

GROSS MOTOR SKILLS
Using of one's large muscles to move (e.g., walking, running, hopping, jumping). [6]

GROUP HOME
Considered a substitute home that is typically located in a residential neighborhood. It provides foster care for orphans, delinquents, disabled persons, or other individuals with special needs. [97]

GUARDIANSHIP
Guardianship is a legal relationship established by the court. It gives a person legal authority over another person if they are deemed unable to make safe and sound decisions regarding his or her person or property. Legal guardianships can involve minor children, developmentally disabled adults, or incapacitated adults. [98]

HEALTHCARE POWER OF ATTORNEY
The *health care power of attorney* is a legal document in which a person can designate someone to be their representative, or agent, in the event they are unable to make or communicate decisions about all aspects of their health care. [99]

HEALTH INSURANCE PORTABILITY AND ACCOUNTABILITY ACT (HIPAA)
HIPAA is a federal privacy law that protects sensitive patient health information from being disclosed without a patient's consent or knowledge. HIPAA laws protect intervention, therapy information, and autism diagnoses. [100]

HIDDEN CURRICULUM
Having an understanding of unwritten or implied social rules and knowing what to do or say in different social situations. It is based on the work of autism researcher Brenda Smith Myles. It is the social information that is not directly taught but is assumed that everybody knows. [24]

HIGH FUNCTIONING AUTISM
A term used to describe autistic individuals who do not have a co-occurring intellectual disability and do not have a cognitive impairment. [4, 54]

HOLISTIC
Encompasses caring for the whole person—providing for physical, mental, spiritual, and social needs. [101]

THE HOME AND COMMUNITY-BASED SERVICES (HCBS) SETTINGS FINAL RULE
This is a federal policy change announced by the Centers for Medicare and Medicaid Services (CMS) in January 2014 to ensure that people with disabilities have the kinds of services they need in their communities. [102]

HYPERACTIVE
Over-active in an abnormal way. [4]

HYPERLEXIA
The ability to read far above and before age or developmental level within the context of another developmental disorder. Children with hyperlexia normally have a very early and strong interest in letters, symbols, and patterns much sooner than is normally seen in children. [103]

HYPERRESPONSIVENESS
The exaggerated responses exhibited by a person after a sensory experience occurs. Hyperresponsiveness is often associated with sensory processing disorders. [104]

HYPERSENSITIVE
Excessive occurrence of sensitivity to sensations or stimuli. 4 Hypersensitivity: Excessive, often painful reactions to daily auditory, visual, or tactile stimuli like bright lights and loud noises. [6]

HYPERTONIA
A condition seen in children characterized by an unusual and abnormal increase in tension impacting muscles of the body. [105]

HYPORESPONSIVENESS
A condition often associated with sensory processing, which refers to limited responses exhibited by a person after a sensory experience has occurred. [106]

HYPOSENSITIVITY
A marked absence of reaction to everyday stimuli. [6]

HYPOTENSION
Low blood pressure. [107]

HYPOTONIA
A medical term describing decreased muscle tone. [108]

IDENTIFICATION
Assessment of a child as a candidate for special education services. Screening and assessment tools are used to confirm if a child has autism or any another disorder. [6]

IDENTITY FIRST LANGUAGE
Language that begins with a person's diagnosis (e.g., being a disabled person). [109]

IDIOSYNCRATIC LANGUAGE
A speech condition that occurs when a person uses familiar words or phrases in a very unusual yet meaningful way. It is a broad term that refers to several speech characteristics where there are errors in communication pragmatics. Idiosyncratic language is a common feature of speech in children with autism and often thought of as stereotypical or an inappropriate word use. The unusual utterances can often include pedantic speech, where a child may use overly specific details. [110]

IMPULSIVE
Reacting and acting out without regard to future consequences. [11]

INCIDENCE
Refers to the number of new cases of an illness or condition occurring in a certain population in a certain time period. [4]

INCLUSION
An educational model where special education students spend as much time as possible in settings with non-special-education students. In the broader context of autism, inclusion can possibly reduce stigma, increase opportunities for social learning, increase encounters with social acceptance, and improve the overall social standing of students with autism. [111]

INCLUSIVE
A term describing the embracement of all people irrespective of race, gender, disability, medical or other need. [112]

INCLUSIVE EDUCATION
A policy in which all students are educated in an academic environment alongside their peers, have equitable access to learning and achievement, and are considered welcomed, valued, and supported in the educational school system. Inclusion promotes participation, friendship, and interaction. [4]

INCONTINENCE
Loss of bladder or bowel control. [6]

INDEPENDENT EDUCATION EVALUATION (IEE)
A type of evaluation performed by an outside licensed professional who isn't employed by a school district. An IEE can determine and decide if a child has a learning disability or other disorder and can identify the best and most appropriate educational services for the child. [113, 114,169]

INDIVIDUAL PLAN FOR EMPLOYMENT (IPE)
A detailed written document created to offer adult individuals with disabilities choices in their planning and outcomes for future employment. An IPE document is a formal plan developed with the help of parents, educators, and participants to decide on a specific vocational goal and the necessary resources to achieve that goal. [115, 169]

INDIVIDUALIZED EDUCATION PROGRAM (IEP)
A guide or plan for a child's academic special education experience at school. It offers individualized special education and related services, like accommodations, to meet a child's individual needs.

The IEP identifies a student's specific learning expectations, goals, objectives and outlines how the school district will meet these expectations through special education programs and services. It also identifies the specific methods by which the student's progress will be measured and reviewed. For students fourteen years or older, it must also contain a specific transitional program for postsecondary education, or the workplace, or to help the student live as independently as possible in the community. [54, 116]

INDIVIDUALIZED FAMILY SERVICE PLAN (IFSP)
A written guide or plan for a child's early intervention services. Think of the IFSP as the foundation for a family's involvement with early intervention programs and services. It explains what services an infant or toddler should receive and what expectations or results the family and support team expect to achieve. [117]

INDIVIDUALIZED TRANSITION PLAN (ITP)
A plan based on informal and formal assessments or evaluations that is often used to identify the desired and expected outcomes or results by students and their families after they leave school along with the supports needed to achieve these desired outcomes. [118]

INDIVIDUALS WITH DISABILITIES EDUCATION ACT (IDEA)
A federal legislative act that ensures all children diagnosed with disabilities are entitled to a free appropriate public education (FAPE) to meet their individual needs and ready them for further education, employment, and independent living. [119]

INFLEXIBILITY
Describes resistance to change or variation. Characteristic of rigid and unyielding in temper, purpose, demeanor, behavior, and/or will. [24]

INTEGRATION
Describes the placement and education of students with disabilities in educational programs that also serve students who do not have disabilities (also referred to as Mainstreaming). [4]

INTELLECTUAL DISABILITY
A diagnosis characterized by impairments in mental abilities, like reasoning, problem-solving, planning, abstract thinking, judgment, academic learning, and learning from experience. The deficits result in impairments of adaptive functioning, such that a person fails to meet standards of personal independence and social responsibility in one or several aspects of daily life. [18]

INTENSIVE BEHAVIORAL INTERVENTION (IBI)
IBI refers to an intensive and comprehensive program of therapeutic treatment for younger children with autism using a systematic Applied Behavioral Analysis approach to teaching. These programs also include speech language therapy and other educational programs that are designed to that of similar behavioral approaches. [4]

IQ (INTELLIGENCE QUOTIENT)
IQ, or intelligence quotient, is the measure of your ability to reason and problem solve. It reflects how well you did on a specific test as compared to other peers in your age group. [120]

INTELLIGENCE SCORE
The measure of an individual's performance on a standardized test of intelligence, based on a comparison of the person's performance to that of many others of the same age performing the same tasks. [4]

INTERDISCIPLINARY TEAM
A collaborative working agreement among professionals to meet the needs of a student, client, or family. [121]

INTERNATIONAL STATISTICAL CLASSIFICATION OF DISEASE AND RELATED HEALTH PROBLEMS (ICD)
A global organization responsible for identifying health trends and statistics globally and the international standard for reporting diseases and health conditions. It is the diagnostic classification standard for all clinical and research purposes. [122]

IRLEN SYNDROME
Visual perceptual problem first identified by Helen Irlen. This syndrome causes (among other things) black-on-white print to be difficult to read and can be alleviated by a process of filtering out portions of the light spectrum with colored glasses. [4]

JOINT ATTENTION
A developmental milestone that involves coordinating eye gaze and focus of attention with that of another individual or person. Delays in joint attention are often an identifier and considered a red flag for the early diagnosis of autism. [123]

KARYOTYPES
The entire and complete set of chromosomes of a cell or organism. [4]

KINESTHETIC
The human sense that detects bodily position, weight, or movement of the muscles, tendons, and joints. [4]

LANGUAGE
The ability to create a thought into a grammatical sequence of verbal or written words. This also includes an ability to utilize an acquired ability receptively and expressively. [4]

LANGUAGE DISORDER
A neurodevelopment condition which includes difficulties or challenges with acquiring and using language. A language disorder may also be classified as a communication disorder and is normally identified in early childhood. Language disorders' core diagnostic features include difficulties acquiring and using language due to deficits in the comprehension or production of vocabulary, sentence structure, and discourse. The language deficits are prevalent in spoken communication, written communication, or sign language. [124]

LEARNING DISABILITY (LD)
A particular category of diagnostic conditions that involve persistent difficulties or deficits in learning critical academic skills, with onset during formal schooling years. Critical academic skills include reading single words accurately and fluently, reading comprehension, written expression and spelling, arithmetic calculations, and mathematical reasoning. [18]

LEAST RESTRICTIVE ENVIRONMENT (LRE)
A component of the Individuals with Disabilities Education Act which requires that children who receive special education learn in the least restrictive environment possible. The provision indicates that all children, whenever possible, should spend time with peers who do not receive special education. It is the requirement in federal and state law that students with disabilities receive their education, to the maximum extent appropriate, with nondisabled peers. [125, 126]

LEITER INTERNATIONAL PERFORMANCE SCALE
A nonverbal scale that measures intellectual functioning and is normed for individuals between two years and twenty years eleven months. [127]

LEVEL OF SUPPORT
Each person with ASD is further diagnosed with either ASD level 1, level 2, or level 3, depending on how severe their disorder is and how much support they need in their daily life. Level one requires support. Level two requires substantial support. Level three requires very substantial support. [128]

LOCAL EDUCATIONAL AGENCY (LEA)
A legal description of the local education authority in a particular region. LEA describes a public board of education or other public

administration legally constituted within a state for either administrative control or direction of, or to perform a service function
for, public elementary schools or secondary schools in a city,
county, township, school district, or other political subdivision of
a state, or for a combination of school districts or counties as are
recognized in a state as an administrative agency for its public
elementary schools or secondary schools. [129]

LOW FUNCTIONING AUTISM
Refers to the condition of children with low level of Intelligence
Quotient (IQ) that is less than a score of 70 who are nonverbal
and have severe autistic symptoms. [4]

MAGNETIC RESONANCE IMAGING (MRI)
A diagnostic test that uses the magnetic qualities of body
chemicals to exhibit an image of the brain. [4]

MAINSTREAMING
An academic and education model describing the placement
of a child with special education needs in a general education
classroom during some or most of the learning day. Placement
of a disabled child with non-disabled peers in a regular classroom. [4, 130]

MAJOR DEPRESSIVE DISORDER (MDD)
Depression is considered a mood disorder that causes a
consistent feeling of sadness and loss of interest in activities. Also
referred to as major depressive disorder or clinical depression,
it affects how you feel, think, and behave. It can lead to a combination of emotional and physical problems. [131, 18]

MASKING

Masking, also referred to as compensating, is considered a social survival strategy. Masking presents differently in individuals and can include behaviors like: forcing or faking eye contact during conversations, imitating smiles or other facial expressions, mimicking gestures, hiding or even minimizing personal interests, developing a repertoire of rehearsed responses to questions, scripting conversations, pushing through intense sensory discomfort like loud noises, disguising stimming behaviors (e.g., hiding a jiggling foot, trading a socially preferred movement for one that's less obvious). [132]

MEDIATION (IN THE CONTEXT OF IEP)

A confidential, voluntary process that allows parties to settle disputes without a formal due process hearing. A mediator, who is impartial to both parties, helps the parties communicate and express their views, positions, and understand each other's' perspectives or positions. The mediator facilitates communication and helps them reach an agreement. The mediator does not recommend solutions or take positions or sides. [133]

MEDICAL ASSISTANCE/MEDICAID (MA)

Medicaid health insurance provides health coverage to many Americans, including low-income adults, children, pregnant women, elderly adults, and people with disabilities. Medicaid is administered by all fifty states, according to federal legislative requirements. The program is funded by both state and federal governments. [134]

MEDICAL HOME

The American Academy of Pediatrics refers to the medical home as a model of delivering primary care that is considered accessible, continuous, comprehensive, family-centered, coordinated, compassionate, and culturally effective. [4]

MELATONIN
A hormone that impacts the immune system and aids in controlling someone's sleep cycle. Sometimes it is given to children who have trouble sleeping at night. [4]

MELTDOWN
Meltdowns frequently happen as an intense response to situations when an individual becomes totally overwhelmed by their circumstance or environment. Sometimes they may temporarily lose all sense of behavioral control. This loss of control can be exhibited several ways: verbally (e.g., shouting, screaming, crying), physically (e.g., kicking, lashing out, biting), or in a combination of both ways. [135]

MENTAL AGE (MA)
An assessment of intellectual functioning based on the average standard for children of the same chronological age. [6]

MENTAL RETARDATION
A medical term referring to significantly below average intelligence (IQ of 70 or less), which onsets or manifests during the critical developmental period and coexists with impairments in adaptive behavior. [4]

METACOGNITION
Personal knowledge and understanding of your very own unique thinking. [137] [136]

MINDFULNESS

The basic human ability to be completely and fully present, aware of where we are and what we're doing, and not overly reactive, stimulated, or overwhelmed by what's going on around us. [137]

MOBILE THERAPY

A relatively new concept involving smartphones or text messaging to provide treatment for certain psychological conditions. [138]

MOBILITY

The ability to physically move around and engage in work or exercise. [4]

MODELING

The act of learning behavior by the observation of others. A professional can "model" a specific treatment for someone on a support team to copy and repeat. [4]

MODIFIED CHAT (M-CHAT)

An empirically validated developmental screening tool designed for toddlers between sixteen months and thirty months of age. The M-CHAT identifies children who may benefit from a more thorough developmental and autism evaluation. [139]

MODULATION

A process of self-regulating physical responses to external stimuli. [11]

MOTOR PLANNING

The ability to think through and physically complete a task. This involves the ability to create the idea of an action, organize it, and then execute it:

- Forming the idea
- Developing the idea to achieve the goal (e.g., what do I want or need to do here?)
- Organizing
- Coordinating the body to prepare for achieving the goal (e.g., deciding what the body has to do and how)
- Execution
- Performing the action (e.g., doing it). [4,6]

NATURAL ENVIRONMENT
The home and other community or environmental settings in which children and their families typically participate in activities. [4]

NATURAL LANGUAGE PARADIGM (NLP)
Note: NLP is also an acronym for something else: "Neuro-Linguistic Programming", which is why "Natural Language Paradigm" has been renamed as "Pivotal Response Training." (See Pivotal Response Training). [4]

NEUROBIOLOGICAL
An adjective referring to the branch of life sciences which deals with the anatomy, physiology, and pathology of the nervous system. [4]

NEURODIVERSE
An idea that people experience and interact with the world around them in a variety of different ways; there is no one "right" way of thinking, learning, and behaving. Differences are not viewed as deficits. [140]

NEURODIVERGENT
Possessing an atypical neurological configuration. [141]

NEURODIVERSITY
The idea that neurological differences such as autism, ADHD, Anxiety, Depression, Dyslexia can result from normal variations in the human genome. Neurodiversity represents a new and fundamentally alternate way of looking at certain conditions as a different way of thinking and processing information, rather than something being considered impaired or having an impairment. It is noted for having an "Increased tolerance for behaviors and cognitions due to hypothesized differential wiring. A social movement towards inclusion." (verbal quote by Sean Inderbitzen) [124, 143]

NEUROHERESY
"Theories of autism not pertaining to differential wiring." (verbal quote by Sean Inderbitzen) [144]

NEUROLOGIST
A doctor specializing in the field of neurology. Neurology is the branch of medicine concerned with the study and treatment of disorders of the nervous system. The nervous system is a complex, sophisticated system that regulates and coordinates body activities. [145]

NEURO-MOTOR
A process involving both nervous system and muscles. [6]

NEUROPLASTICITY
The ability of the neural networks in our brain to change and grow through experiences in the environment. The argument for Early Intervention services stems from the concept of

neuroplasticity and that individuals with ASD can overcome interfering symptoms through 'rewiring' of the neural networks at a young age. [146]

NEUROTRANSMITTER
The chemical in the brain which transmits messages every day from one nerve cell to another nerve cell. [4]

NEUROTYPICAL (NT)
A word commonly used to describe the majority of individuals who experience the world in a different and more prevalent way. The term 'neurotypical' implies the absence of a neurodivergent profile (see also Neurodiversity). [147]

NO CHILD LEFT BEHIND ACT (NCLB)
A federally regulated legislative act signed under the George W. Bush administration. No Child Left Behind's primary focus is to close student achievement gaps by providing all children with a fair, equal, and significant opportunity to obtain a high-quality education. [148]

NONVERBAL COMMUNICATION
Any form of communication that does not involve the use of verbally spoken language. (e.g., gestures, facial expressions, eye contact). [4]

NONVERBAL LEARNING DISORDER OR NONVERBAL LEARNING DISABILITY (NLD or NVLD)
An educational term, not included as a formal psychiatric diagnosis in the DSM-5. AS/ASD is a nonverbal learning difference, but some people with NLD share only *some* traits with people with AS/ASD.

A nonverbal learning disability describes a situation in which the underlying cause of a student's learning difficulties is believed to be a generalized weakness in the ability to cognitively process nonverbal information. Typically, such a student performs quite well verbally (both receptively or "listening" and expressively or "speaking") but struggles to understand or remember information which is presented visually. This is not due to poor vision but is related to an assumed weakness in the brain's ability to fully or efficiently process nonverbal information. [4, 24]

NOTICE OF RECOMMENDED EDUCATIONAL PLACEMENT (NOREP)

A form completed at the end of developing an Individualized Education Program (IEP) for a student receiving special education services in an academic setting. The NOREP must be provided to parents when a school district or other educational entity proposes a change to the student's program or placement at the school. The NOREP form summarizes the student's educational placement and explains the parents' rights to agree or disagree to such proposed changes. [149]

OBJECTIVES

The intermediate steps in an IEP that must be taken to reach a student's annual goals. [6]

OBSESSIONS

Recurrent and persistent thoughts, urges, or images experienced as intrusive and unwired and that in most individuals cause marked anxiety or distress. The individual may attempt to ignore or suppress such thoughts, urges, or images or neutralize them with some other thought or action. [18]

OBSESSIVE COMPULSIVE DISORDER (OCD)

A diagnosis characterized by the presence of obsession, compulsions, or both. Obsessions are recurrent and persistent thoughts, urges, or images experienced as intrusive and unwanted. In contrast, compulsions are repetitive behaviors or mental acts that an individual feels driven to perform in response to an obsession or according to rules that must be applied rigidly. Many individuals with autism demonstrate OCD-type behaviors or may have a co-diagnosis of OCD. [18]

OCCUPATIONAL PERFORMANCE

The ability to choose, organize and effectively and safely complete everyday activities which are necessary for self-care and daily participation in educational, leisure, home management, and work activities. [4]

OCCUPATIONAL THERAPIST (OT)

Individuals who specialize in the analysis of activity and tasks to minimize the impact of a disability on activities of daily living. The therapist also helps the family members to better adapt, and cope with the disorder, by adapting the environment and teaching. [4]

OCCUPATIONAL THERAPY (OT)

An evidence-based intervention for autism as well as other conditions. OT helps people across the lifespan do the things they want and need to do through the therapeutic use of daily activities (occupations). Occupational therapy practitioners enable people of all ages to live life to its fullest quality of life by helping them promote health and prevent—or live better with—injury, illness, or disability. [150]

OFFICE FOR CIVIL RIGHTS (OCR)
A federal agency under the jurisdiction of the Department of Health and Human Services (DHHS). OCR's mission is to ensure equal access to education and promote educational excellence through vigorous enforcement of civil rights in United States schools. [151]

OFFICE FOR DISPUTE RESOLUTION
A federal agency under the jurisdiction of the Department of Justice. Office of Dispute Resolution is part of the Department of Justice's Office of Legal Policy. The Office of Dispute Resolution's mission is to develop policy and promote the effective use of alternative dispute resolution ("ADR") processes. [152]

OPPOSITIONAL DEFIANT DISORDER (ODD):
A diagnosis characterized by frequent and persistent patterns of angry/irritable mood, argumentative/defiant behavior, or vindictiveness. Oppositional Defiant Disorder is listed in the *Diagnostic and Statistical Manual* (DSM-5) under disruptive, impulse-control, and conduct disorders. Children with ODD engage in similar behaviors as other conduct disorders, but they are not aggressive at all towards people or animals, do not destroy property, and do not show a theft or deceit pattern. [18]

ORAL MOTOR
Movements of the face muscles (e.g., mouth, jaw, tongue, lips). Oral motor behaviors can include chewing, biting, speaking, and singing. Delays in oral motor development may have an impact on muscle tone, muscle strength, range of motion, speed, coordination, and dissociation (the ability to move oral structures, such as the tongue and lip, independently of each other). [153]

ORTHOPEDIC IMPAIRMENT

A condition in which severe orthopedic impairment adversely affects a child's educational performance at school. The term includes impairments caused by congenital anomaly (e.g., clubfoot, absence of some member), impairments caused by disease (e.g., poliomyelitis, bone tuberculosis), or impairments from other specified causes (e.g., cerebral palsy, amputations, fractures or burns that cause contractures). [154]

PANTER FORM

A document used by B.C.'s Ministry of Health, Ministry of Children and Family Development and Community Living BC. A form, which must be completed by a child's pediatrician, neurologist, psychiatrist or registered psychologist. This medically validated and signed form confirms that a multidisciplinary assessment has been completed by a professional and that the child has autism spectrum disorder. [4]

PARAPROFESSIONAL

Educational personnel are also referred to as teacher aides, educational or classroom aides. Whether in general education classrooms or special classes, paraprofessionals can assist and provide meaningful support to students with disabilities. [4]

PARASYMPATHETIC NERVOUS SYSTEM

A part of the nervous system that regulates automatic (nonvoluntary)bodily functions. [155]

PATHOLOGICAL DEMAND AVOIDANCE (PDA)

A profile that describes individuals whose main exhibited characteristic is to avoid everyday demands and expectations to a very extreme extent. Pathological demand avoidance (PDA) was a term first used by Professor Elizabeth Newson in the 1980s, that described a group of children she had seen for assessment. PDA is increasingly, but not universally, accepted as a profile that is seen in some autistic people. It is not recognized by the DSM-5. [156, 157]

PEDIATRIC AUTOIMMUNE NEUROPSYCHIATRIC DISORDERS ASSOCIATED WITH STREPTOCOCCAL INFECTIONS (PANDAS)

A neurological and psychiatric condition in which symptoms are onset or worsened by a Streptococcal (strep) infection. [158]

PEER-MEDIATED INTERVENTION (PMI)

Any instruction or intervention for a child with ASD implemented with another child without disabilities. Peer-mediated interventions are an evidence-based practice for teaching a variety of skills to children with ASD, including language, social behaviors, and daily living behaviors. PMI may include class-wide interventions, peer modeling, peer tutoring, or social skills training. [159]

PERCEPTUAL PROBLEMS

Difficulty in interpreting sensory information. Also includes difficulty making sense of the environment. [4]

PERFORMANCE IQ

The score derived from several nonverbal tests, such as visual-spatial activities and object assembly. [6]

PERSEVERATE

To repeat something insistently or redundantly. Perseveration occurs when someone gets stuck on a topic or an idea. [160]

PERSEVERATION

A set of behaviors marked by persistence in tasks or in a particular way of doing things long after the behavior has ceased to be functional or effective—continuance of the same behavior despite repeated failures or apparent reason for stopping. [18]

PERVASIVE DEVELOPMENTAL DISORDER (PDD) OR PERVASIVE DEVELOPMENTAL DISORDER—NOT OTHERWISE SPECIFIED (PDD-NOS):

A diagnostic label that was formerly used to describe individuals with developmental delays on the Autism spectrum. PDD and PDD-NOS (not otherwise specified) were eliminated with the publication of the DSM-5 due to difficulties reliably identifying the communication and social deficits of PDD separately from those of individuals with ASD. At this time, all individuals who meet the diagnostic criteria receive a diagnosis of autism. 161 Person-Centered Planning: Person-centered planning (PCP) is a process for selecting and organizing certain services and supports that an older adult or person with a disability may need to live independently in the community. [4]

PHYSICAL THERAPY (PT)

An evidence-based therapy for the preservation, enhancement, or restoration of movement and physical function impaired or threatened by illness, disease, injury, or disability. Many individuals with autism receive PT services as part of their treatment plan. [162]

PICA

A condition involving eating one or more nonnutritive, nonfood substances on an ongoing basis for at least one month that is severe enough to warrant clinical attention. Typical substances ingested tend to vary with age and availability and might include paper, soap, cloth, hair, string, wool, soil, chalk, talcum powered, paint, gum, metal, pebbles, charcoal, coal ash, clay, starch, or ice. [18]

PICTURE EXCHANGE COMMUNICATION SYSTEM (PECS)

A communication system helping people with little or no vocal speech to communicate using a system of pictures. People using PECS are taught to approach another person and give them a picture of the desired item in exchange for that item. [163]

PIVOTAL RESPONSE TRAINING

An evidence-based and naturalistic intervention model derived from Applied Behavior Analysis (ABA). Pivotal Response Training emphasizes using child motivation to teach responses within play along with other social activities. [164]

POLYVAGAL THEORY

Stephen Porge's Polyvagal Theory proposes the evolution of the mammalian autonomic nervous system provides the neurophysiological substrates for adaptive behavioral strategies. [165]

POSITIVE BEHAVIOR SUPPORT (PBS)

The broad enterprise of helping people develop and engage in adaptive, socially desirable behaviors and overcome patterns of destructive and stigmatizing responding. Unlike traditional behavioral management, which views the individual as the problem and seeks to "fix" him or her by quickly eliminating the challenging behavior, positive behavioral support (PBS) and functional analysis (FA) view systems, settings, and lack of skill as parts of the "problem" and work to change those. As such, these approaches are characterized as long-term strategies to reduce inappropriate behavior, teach more appropriate behavior, and provide contextual supports necessary for successful outcomes. PBS and FA can help practitioners and parents understand why the challenging behavior occurs—its function or purpose for the individual. In addition to helping practitioners and families understand the individual with the challenging behavior, PBS and FA also help them understand the physical and social contexts of the behavior. Moreover, PBS and FA provide a framework for helping the child to change challenging behaviors. [54]

PRADER-WILLI SYNDROME
A rare genetic disorder caused by loss of genetic functioning on the paternally derived genes of chromosome 15. About twenty percent of individuals with Prader-Willi syndrome also have a diagnosis of ASD and are impacted by similar behavioral and social difficulties. [167]

PRAGMATICS
A term used to describe the acquisition of knowledge needed for daily language in appropriate and effective social contexts. DSM-5 defines this as the understanding and use of language in a given context. [167, 18]

PREOCCUPATION WITH PARTS OF OBJECTS
A repetitive or ritualistic behavior characteristic of some with autism. Some individuals with autism may also become attached to certain objects (or parts of objects) Examples include toys, figurines, model cars, or more unusual things like Thomas the Train, bottle tops, rocks, or shoes. Also, having an interest in collecting things is also quite common. [168]

PRESENT LEVEL OF PERFORMANCE (PLOP, PLP, PLAFF, PLAAFP)
This is a current view of how a child is currently doing based on performance. PLOP describes a child's academic skills (e.g., reading level) and functional skills (e.g., making conversation, writing with a pencil). The school the child attends will prepare

this report for preparation for an upcoming IEP meeting. This is the very beginning benchmark or starting point for establishing annual IEP goals. [169]

PRESENT LEVELS OF ACADEMIC ACHIEVEMENT AND FUNCTIONAL PERFORMANCE (PLAAFP)

The Present Levels of Academic Achievement and Functional Performance statement (PLAAFP, or "present levels") is a very important part of a child's Individualized Education Program (IEP). The very first PLAAFP for a child describes their skills and abilities based on their initial special education evaluation. [170]

PREVALENCE

The proportion of people with a specific condition or disease within a particular population at a given time. For example, the prevalence of autism spectrum disorder is 1 in 44. [4]

PRIOR WRITTEN NOTICE

A formal letter that a school sends to a child's parents. This is also considered a legal right under IDEA. If a school district takes any action to deny, refuse, or accept a parent's request for an evaluation or a change to a special education service, it must provide a prior written notice. [169]

PROCESSING

Cognitive operations; the act of thinking. [4]

PROGNOSIS

The possible outcome or outcomes of a particular condition or a disease that includes the likelihood that each one will occur based on a medical model of treatment. [4]

PROPRIOCEPTIVE OR PROPRIOCEPTION
A formulated sense of body awareness created by interpreting the information from the muscles and joints. [4]

PROSODY
A term related to speech which describes intonation, stress pattern, loudness variations, pausing, and rhythm. Prosody is mainly described by varying pitch, loudness, and duration. Some individuals with autism may have atypical prosody. They may also receive specific interventions to help others more easily understand speech. [171]

PROTODECLARATIVE POINTING
A communicative gesture mainly used to establish social interaction and direct a caregiver's focus towards an object, action, or entity. Protodeclarative pointing points attention to a specific object, action, or entity by the child as a communicative exchange or comment. A protodeclarative may also take several gestural forms, including pointing to, showing, or giving objects. The gesture can sometimes be accompanied by a type of ritualized vocalization. [172]

PROTOIMPERATIVE POINTING
A type of communicative gesture used by a person to obtain an object or to obtain some state of affairs in the physical world. 173 Psychiatrist: Doctor trained and certified to prescribe medications. [11]

PUBLIC LAW 94-142
A federal legislative act, also referred to as the Education for All Handicapped Children Act (EAHCA) of 1975. The law pertains to the education of children with disabilities and it guarantees

a "free, appropriate public education" to all children and young adults ages three to twenty-one (see also FAPE). [174]

The Education of All Handicapped Children Act of 1975, ratified again in 2004, providing a "free, appropriate public education" for every child with a diagnosed disability. [6]

RECEPTIVE LANGUAGE
The comprehension, processing, input, or receiving of language. Receptive language describes the ability to understand information that is being communicated. It involves understanding meanings and functions of spoken and written words. Receptive language tasks often involve identifying specific items from an array and following accompanying instructions. [6, 175]

RECEPTIVE LANGUAGE DISORDER
A subcategory of communication disorders that primarily concern deficits in language comprehension and following verbal instructions. [176]

REGISTRY OF SERVICE PROVIDERS FOR THE AUTISM FUNDING (RASP)
The list identifies service providers who have applied and been accepted to be placed on a registry in order to provide treatment services for children with autism spectrum disorder. This program is for children ages six and under and is maintained by ACT: Autism Community Training. [4]

REGRESSION
Regression refers to a reversion of an earlier mental or behavioral level. Regressive autism can be subsequently diagnosed when a child who met developmental milestones up to those of fifteen to thirty months old, who show signs of losing skills in language and social areas. [177]

REGULATION
"The state of being controlled or governed." [4]

REINFORCEMENT
A principle of Applied Behavior Analysis (ABA) and operant conditioning where enforcement describes a naturally occurring process by which a specific consequence is delivered immediately after a specific behavior increases the frequency of that same response occurring in the future. Positive reinforcement is the foundation of ABA therapy. [178]

RELATED SERVICES
Additional services most often considered to be a part of an Individualized Education Program (IEP) and special education services. [180]

RELATIONSHIP DEVELOPMENT INTERVENTION (RDI)
RDI is considered a family-centered treatment program for individuals with autism. RDI focuses primarily on building social and emotional skills with parents and caregivers as the primary practitioner. RDI has six objectives: emotional referencing, social coordination, declarative language, flexible thinking, relational information processing, foresight, and hindsight. [180]

REPETITIVE BEHAVIORS AND RESTRICTED INTERESTS
Repetitive behaviors and restricted interests are considered one of the core diagnostic features of Autism Spectrum Disorders. Repetitive behavior can often include arm- or hand-flapping, finger-flicking, rocking, jumping, spinning or twirling, head-banging, and making complex body movements. Repetitive behaviors may also involve using an object, such as flicking a

rubber band or twisting a piece of string, or repetitive activities involving the senses (such as repeatedly feeling a particular texture). Some of these behaviors may also be referred to as 'stimming,' or self-stimulating behavior. Restricted interests include fixation on specific topics, conversations, or themes. Repetitive behaviors and restricted interests may be considered lifelong for individuals with ASD or may change and evolve over time. [181]

REPRESENTATIVE PAYEE

A representative payee is a person or an organization appointed a payee to receive the Social Security or SSI benefits for individuals who can't manage their own financial benefits.

RESPITE CARE

Short-term relief provided by someone for primary caregivers. Respite care often involves personal care assistance (PCA), home health care, or nannying service. Depending on eligibility requirements, an insurance or government funding may pay for respite care services. [4, 183]

RESPONSE TO INTERVENTION (RTI)

A method in an educational setting that identifies and matches struggling students with tools to succeed in school. Characteristics can include things like assessment, early identification, and targeted interventions. RTI programs often involve data collection and positive reinforcement components. [184]

REVERSE MAINSTREAMING OR REVERSE MAINSTREAM

An educational practice that places children without disabilities into special education settings. Peers often join a classroom or a therapy session for a specific timeframe for the purpose of implementing targeted goals or to promote positive social inter-action. Professionals often implement reverse mainstreaming to improve the daily contact between children in special education settings and their more typical peers. Reverse Mainstreaming allows the special education students an opportunity to engage with their neuro-typical peers without leaving their highly struc-tured and individualized educational settings. [4, 185]

RISPERDAL
A type of pharmaceutical medication usually prescribed to treat problematic behaviors like aggression, self-injury, and irrita-bility in children, adolescents, and adults with autism. The drug improves symptoms by reducing abnormal excitement in the brain. [4]

RITUALS
While often considered neither purposeful nor problematic, certain ritualistic behaviors can also be considered as functional behavior for individuals with autism. [186]

RYAN'S LAW
A law that was passed by the SC legislature in 2007 which required certain types of businesses to cover ABA therapy through their insurance plans. [188]

SCERT'S MODEL
A comprehensive, multidisciplinary educational model developed by Barry Prizant and Emily Rubin in order to address the many needs of students with autism and related challenges. The acronym stands for Social Communication, Emotional Regulation, Transactional Support, which are the cornerstones of this approach. This approach is used for improving communication and socioemotional abilities for young children with an autism diagnosis. [4,6]

SCREENING
A process that examines whether a child is meeting developmental milestones at age-appropriate timeframes. Children may be administered a brief skills test, or parents may be asked to complete a questionnaire. The tools used for developmental and behavioral screenings often involve formal questionnaires or checklists based on empirical research. Screenings collect data about a child's development such as language, movement, thinking, behavior, and emotions. Developmental screening can be completed by a doctor or nurse and other professionals in healthcare, community, or school settings. [188]

SECRETIN
A hormone responsible for controlling digestion, increasing the volume and bicarbonate content of secreted pancreatic juices. [4]

SEIZURES
A burst of uncontrolled electrical activity between cells in the brain, also referred to as neurons or nerve cells. Seizures can cause temporary abnormalities in muscle tone or movements (i.e., stiffness, twitching, or limpness), behaviors, sensations, or states of awareness. Seizure disorders can occur at higher rates in individuals with ASD than in other populations. [189]

SELECTIVE MUTISM

An anxiety disorder characterized by a deficit of speech in one or more contexts or social settings. It is considered a rare disorder that occurs more commonly in females than males. Children with selective mutism exhibit typical patterns and use of speech in "safe" settings, like with family or with close peers. Selective mutism occurs at much higher rates in individuals with autism than in other populations. [18]

SELECTIVE SEROTONIN REUPTAKE INHIBITOR (SSRI)

A certain class of medication used as antidepressants. Typically, they raise the levels of serotonin in the body. These drugs can be considered dangerous if mixed with other drugs such like antidepressants, illicit drugs, some antihistamines, antibiotics and calcium-channel blockers. Some examples of SSRIs are Prozac, Zoloft, and Paxil. [4]

SELF-ADVOCACY

When an individual perceives or expresses their own feelings. It also relates to understanding and accepting one's own strengths and weaknesses. Learning strategies to offset weaknesses and build on strengths. Understanding when one needs help and asking for help appropriately. Recognizing and protecting oneself from circumstances where bullying could occur. [24]

SELF-HELP SKILLS

A subset of a more extensive repertoire of daily living skillsets, sometimes referred to as activities of daily living. Self-help skills include daily activities like feeding, dressing, and independent toileting. [190]

SELF-INJURIOUS BEHAVIOR (SIB)
Behaviors that can result in physical harm to one's own body. Examples of self-injurious behaviors can include headbanging on floors, walls, or other surfaces, hand- or arm-biting, hair-pulling, eye-gouging, face- or head-slapping, skin-picking, scratching, pinching, or forceful head-shaking. SIB may also be referred to as self-harm. Autistic individuals may engage in SIB for various reasons, including but not limited to: sensory input, escape from or avoidance of aversive things in the environment, or obtainment of access to attention or preferred items. Self-injurious behavior often requires professional interventions and treatment. [4, 191]

SELF-MONITORING
Behaviors individuals use to help increase, identify, evaluate, and change behavior without social support from others. Self-monitoring occurs in all healthy adults as part of well-developed executive functioning skills. Many individuals with autism need to be taught self-monitoring skills (e.g., managing and accessing one's own behavior to promote self-regulation, independence, and generalization of skills to new settings). [192]

SELF-REGULATION
Behaviors that assist a person in managing their behavior or emotions in social settings. Self-regulation skills can include activities like monitoring and controlling impulsive behavior, adjusting behavior to meet the social context, and communicating one's needs in challenging environments. [193]

SELF-STIMULATORY BEHAVIOR—"STIMMING"
One of the primary diagnostic features of Autism Spectrum Disorder. It often includes stereotyped or repetitive motor movements that are considered an adaptive mechanism, often thought to assist individuals with autism to self-soothe or

communicate intense emotions and thoughts. Self-stimulatory behaviors differ for each individual. [194]

SEMANTIC-PRAGMATIC DISORDER (OR SEMANTIC-PRAGMATIC LANGUAGE IMPAIRMENT)

Children with Semantic-Pragmatic Language Disorder have a hard time understanding the meaning of words and sentences (semantics) and difficulties with the social use of language (pragmatics). They often encounter particular problems in understanding abstract words and concepts or figures of speech and understanding the main idea in a sentence or conversation. Other concerns may arise like problems with turn-taking in conversations, reading the nonverbal cues of their conversational partners, or maintaining a topic or changing topics appropriately. [4]

SENSORIMOTOR

Pertains to brain activity other than automatic functions (respiration, circulation, sleep) or cognition. Sensorimotor activity also includes voluntary movement and senses like sight, touch, and hearing. [4,6]

SENSORY-BASED BEHAVIORS

Behaviors that are a direct result of a child's attempt to meet a sensory need. [4]

SENSORY DEFENSIVENESS

A condition where an individual is highly sensitive to light touch. This type of over-stimulation in the brain can make it difficult for an individual to organize one's behavior and concentrate and may lead to a negative emotional response to touch sensations. [4]

SENSORY DIET
Sensory diets can be used as part of sensory integration therapy. Completing a sensory diet routine can assist children to assist them with paying more attention in school, learn new skills, and socializing with other kids. Sensory diets are often paired with occupational and physical therapy. They have been known to be included in Individualized Education Programs (IEPs). [195]

SENSORY HYPERSENSITIVITIES
Highly sensitive to stimulus being received via the senses (e.g., Touch, Smell, Taste, Sight). [4]

SENSORY INPUT
Environmental stimulation of one of the five primary senses involving the body acquiring information by sight, smell, hearing, taste, and touch. [196]

SENSORY INTEGRATION
The processes in the brain that take the information received from the five primary senses, organize it, and responds appropriately. Sensory integration provides an understanding of the body's nervous system and the accompanying behaviors that are often attempts by the individual to cope with and adapt to nervous system disorganization. [4, 197]

SENSORY INTEGRATION THERAPY (SIT)
Sensory Integration Therapy (SIT) is an evidence-based therapy intervention designed for individuals with ASD and sensory processing challenges. SIT aims to help kids with sensory processing issues (which some individuals may refer to as "sensory integration disorder") by exposing them to sensory stimulation in a structured, repetitive manner. The brain will adapt over time and allow children to process and react to

sensations more efficiently. SIT professionals often recommend a diet of sensory activities (see also Sensory Diet). [4, 197]

SENSORY MODALITY
The way in which a person receives input or information through their senses (proprioceptive, vestibular, visual, tactile, auditory, gustatory, olfactory). [11]

SENSORY MODULATION
Occurs when the senses work together. Every sense works with the others and forms a composite picture of who we are physically, where we are, and what is going on around us. It is considered a neurological function that is responsible for producing this composite picture. [4]

SENSORIMOTOR
Activities that involve learning by means of movement and the senses. [6]

SENSORIMOTOR PSYCHOTHERAPY
Sensorimotor Psychotherapy (SP) is a complete therapeutic modality for trauma and attachment issues that welcomes the body as a source of information. SP is a holistic approach that includes somatic, emotional, and cognitive processing and integration. [198]

SENSORY PROCESSING DISORDER (SPD)
A condition in which the brain has difficulty receiving and responding to information through the five primary senses. SPD differs from sensory integration disorder which is a specific medical condition in which a child has a biological difference resulting in changes to receiving and responding to sensory input, like seeing, hearing, smelling, tasting, and touching. [199]

SENSORY REGULATION
The ability of a person to integrate external stimuli into their personal experience or experiences. [24]

SENSORY SENSITIVITIES
Describes hypersensitivity or hyposensitivity to sights, sounds, smells, tastes, touch, balance, and body awareness. Individuals with autism may exhibit more sensory sensitivities than other populations. [200]

SENSORY STIMULATION
Describes the sensations an individual might often hear, see, or feel that can lead to certain behaviors in an environment. [201]

SEROTONIN
A neurotransmitter, i.e., brain chemical that plays a part in communication within the nervous system. It has been noted that the level of serotonin measured in autistic people is sometimes higher than that in typical people. [4]

SERVICE ANIMAL
A working animal—often a dog—that has been trained to perform specific tasks to assist individuals with disabilities. Service animals can support individuals with ASD in a variety of ways, including accompanying and assisting with community activities, interrupting self-harm, deescalating meltdowns, and preventing elopement. [202]

SERVICE COORDINATOR
A single point of contact for a family responsible for coordinating services that can be delivered by multiple service providers. Service coordinators are educated about community resources that may be available to help meet the needs of the family. [203]

SHARED ATTENTION AND MEANING
Also called Joint Attention, occurs when a child and play partner are both focused on the same theme, object, and/or idea. [4]

SLOW PROCESSING DISORDER
The inability for the brain to digest information and then react to the information at the expected speed. This can often result in delayed reactions to questions. [11]

SOCIAL COMMUNICATION
A language subset which involves three significant areas of skills: using language for different reasons, changing language for the listener or situation, and following specific rules for conversation or storytelling. [204]

SOCIAL COMMUNICATION DISORDER (SCD)
A disorder characterized by a persistent difficulty with both verbal and nonverbal communication that cannot be simply explained by low cognitive ability. Symptoms often will include difficulty in the acquisition and use of spoken and written language and problems with inappropriate responses in conversation. The disorder can cause deficits in effective communication, social relationships, academic achievement, or occupational performance. Symptoms must be presented in early childhood, even if they are not recognizable until later, when speech, language, or communication demands exceed abilities. [18]

SOCIAL EMOTIONAL LEARNING (SEL)
Social and emotional learning (SEL) is a vital part of education and human development. SEL is a process by which young people and adults acquire and apply the knowledge, skills, and attitudes to develop very healthy identities, manage their emotions and achieve personal and collective goals, feel and show empathy

for others, establish and maintain supportive relationships, and make better responsible and caring decisions. [205]

SOCIAL IMITATIVE PLAY
When a child plays and begins to copy or mimic another individual. Delays in social imitative play may be considered a big red flag for the early detection of autism in toddlers. [206]

SOCIAL INTERACTION
A set of behaviors that describes how people engage with other people and responds to the actions of others. [207]

SOCIAL RECIPROCITY
A set of behaviors describing the back-and-forth interactions between people, during which each individual's behavior influences the other person's behavior. [208]

SOCIAL SKILLS
The skills we use every day to interact and communicate with each other. These include verbal and nonverbal communication, like speech, gesture, facial expression, and body language. [209]

SOCIAL PRAGMATICS
Describes having the ability to: Read the room. Notice and correctly interpret other people's nonverbal communication (gestures, body position, facial expression, tone of voice). Modulate one's own nonverbal communication. Initiate, join, and maintain conversation. Listen. Use humor and sarcasm appropriately; understand other people's use of sarcasm and humor. [24]

SOCIAL STORIES™
Social Stories™ were first developed in 1991 by Carol Gray. They were designed as a tool for teaching social skills to kids

with autism. Social Stories™ focus on developing an ability to recognize feelings, various points of view or plans of others. Stories are developed to meet a child's individual needs based on their anxieties, their fears, or the difficulty of particular situations. The stories help children to develop more appropriate responses to real life situations. [4]

SPECIAL EDUCATION (SPED)
Special education provided by a school district focuses on providing a child with an education, regardless of any disabilities or special needs. [4, 6, 211]

SPECIAL INTERESTS
Interests that are deep and narrow and that reflect the heightened and exceptional unique abilities to autism. Special interests could include systemizing or the drive to analyze, explore, and construct a system. [210]

SPECIAL NEEDS ADVOCATE
A professional that is familiar with special needs rules and laws who can assist you in getting services for your child. [11]

SPECIAL NEEDS TRUST (SNT)
A particular legal trust that preserves the beneficiary's eligibility for needs-based government benefits (Medicaid and Supplemental Security Income (SSI)). Because the beneficiary does not own the assets in the trust, he or she can remain eligible for benefit programs that have an asset limit. [212]

SPECIAL OLYMPICS
A global movement of people cultivating a sense of inclusion and community, where every single person is accepted and welcomed, regardless of ability or disability. [213]

SPECIALLY DESIGNED INSTRUCTION (SDI)
An education and therapeutic method; includes adapting, as is appropriate, to an eligible child's needs by modifying or accommodating the content, methodology, or delivery of instruction. [214]

SPECTRUM DISORDER
A disorder that covers a range from mild to severe. [4]

SPEECH THERAPY
A therapeutic and evidence-based method used to treat impairments and disorders of speech, voice, language, communication, and swallowing. [215]

SPEECH-LANGUAGE PATHOLOGIST (SLP)
A medical professional that helps to prevent, assess, diagnose, and treat speech, language, social communication, cognitive-communication, and swallowing disorders in children and adults. [216]

SPLINTER SKILL
A highly specialized skill. Savant gifts, or splinter skills, may be presented in the following skill areas: memory, hyperlexia (i.e., the exceptional ability to read, spell, and write), art, music, mechanical or spatial skill, calendar calculation, mathematical calculation, sensory sensitivity, athletic performance, and computer ability. [217]

SPOONS
A disability metaphor often used to describe and explain the reduced amount of mental and physical energy available for activities for living and productive tasks that can result from disability or chronic illness. [218]

STANDARDS-BASED IEP

An alternative to a traditional IEP that is only used in some states. A standards-based IEP measures a student's individual academic performance against what the state expects of other students in the same grade. [169]

STEREOTYPIES

The constant repetition of certain meaningless movements or gestures (e.g., rocking or head-banging). [4]

STEREOTYPED BEHAVIORS

Behaviors displayed by someone (with autism, for example) that are repeated many times. [4]

STEREOTYPIC MOVEMENT DISORDER

A condition that is typified by a variety of repetitive and uncontrolled movements for a period of no less than four weeks. Certain examples may include body-rocking, head-banging, nail-biting, tics, self-mutilating actions such as self-hitting or picking at one's skin, hand-waving or -wringing, and mouthing an object; all of which interfere with regular daily activities and are potentially harmful. [219]

STIGMA

A social behavior where an individual views others negatively due to a distinguishing characteristic or personal trait that's thought to be, or is, a disadvantage (a negative stereotype). [220]

STIM OR STIMMING

Short for 'self-stimulation,' a term for behaviors whose sole purpose appears to be to stimulate one's senses. Many people with autism report that some 'self-stims' may serve a regulatory function for them (e.g., calming, increasing concentration, or shutting out an overwhelming sound). [4]

Stimming—or self-stimulatory behavior—is repetitive or unusual body movement or noises. [4, 243]

SUICIDAL IDEATION
Obsessive thoughts about suicide. [11]

SUPPLEMENTARY AIDS AND SERVICES
Supports that can assist and help a child learn in a general education classroom. They can include equipment or assistive technology, like audiobooks or highlighted classroom notes. They can also include training for staff to help them work with your child. [169]

SUPPLEMENTAL SECURITY INCOME (SSI)
A federal program that pays benefits to disabled adults and children who have limited income and resources. [221]

SUPPORTED DECISION MAKING (SDM)
Supported Decision-Making (SDM) allows people with disabilities to make choices about their lives with support from a team of people they choose. Individuals with disabilities choose people they know and trust to be part of a support network to help with decision-making. [223]

SUPPORTED EMPLOYMENT
Work done or completed by people with cognitive, physical, or emotional challenges involving an adapted environment or additional support staff. [6]

SUPPORTED LIVING

Supported Living Services (SLS) allow individuals aged 18 and over to continue living at their family home or independently in a community setting using paid supports to augment available (existing) natural and generic community supports.

SYMBOLIC PLAY

A particular type of play using one or several objects, actions, or ideas to represent other objects, actions, or ideas during play. Delays in symbolic play may be a red flag for the early screening of autism in toddlers and young children. This can also be called "pretend play." [224]

SYMPATHETIC NERVOUS SYSTEM

A part of the nervous system that serves to accelerate the heart rate, constrict blood vessels, and raise blood pressure. [225]

SYNDROME

A certain group of signs and symptoms that may occur together and that characterize a particular abnormality or condition. [6, 227]

SYNESTHESIA

A rare condition often experienced by people on the autism spectrum. An experience goes in through one sensory system and out through another. So a person might hear a sound but experience it as a color. In other words, they may 'hear' the color blue. [226]

TACTILE DEFENSIVENESS

Excessive physical sensitivity to certain textures and sensations. This is a condition in which a person is extremely sensitive to light touch. Theoretically, when the tactile system is immature and working improperly, abnormal neural signals are sent to the cortex in the brain which can interfere with other brain processes. This can cause the brain to feel overly stimulated and may lead to excessive brain activity, which can neither be turned off nor organized. This type of over-stimulation in the brain can make it difficult for an individual to organize one's behavior and concentrate and may lead to a negative emotional response to touch sensations. [4,6]

TACTILE DYSFUNCTION

Dysfunction in the tactile system can be viewed in withdrawing when being touched, refusing to eat certain textured foods and/ or to wear certain types of clothing, complaining about having one's hair or face washed, avoiding getting one's hands dirty (e.g., glue, sand, mud, finger-paint), and using one's fingertips rather than whole hands to manipulate objects. A dysfunctional tactile system may lead to a misperception of touch and/or pain (hyper- or hyposensitive) and may lead to self-imposed isolation, general irritability, distractibility, and hyperactivity. [4]

TACTILE SYSTEM

The tactile system includes nerves under the skin's surface that send information to the brain that includes light touch, pain, temperature, and pressure. These play an important role in perceiving the environment as well as protective reactions for survival. [4]

TANTRUM

A set of non-language behaviors a young child uses to express strong emotions before expressing them in socially acceptable ways. A child may appear totally out of control, but these fits of rage, stomping, screaming, and throwing himself or herself to the floor are a normal part of childhood development. [228]

TASK ANALYSIS

Task analysis is the process of learning about ordinary users by observing them in action to understand in detail how they perform their tasks and achieve their overall intended goals. [229]

TEACCH

A therapeutic approach based on an idea that individuals with autism more effectively use and understand visual cues. It focuses on promoting dependence by using items such as picture schedules to break down tasks step by step. This enables an individual to better comprehend and perform the task independently. This approach more often aids receptive communication and sequential memory. [54, 232]

TEACCH MODEL

A program of services, rather than a teaching method, in which respect for individual differences, respect and inclusion of parents and various professionals and input from individuals with autism are considered in treatment and education. It was developed at the University of North Carolina, Chapel Hill and takes a lifespan approach. [6]

TEFRA MEDICAID

Allows children with disabilities to stay at home with their families and receive care in the community. [230]

TEFRA (Tax Equity and Fiscal Responsibility Act of 1982) gives states the option to make Medicaid (SoonerCare) benefits available to children with severe physical or mental disabilities, who would not ordinarily be eligible for Supplemental Security Income (SSI) benefits because of their parent's income or resources. This option allows children who are eligible for institutional services to be cared for in their homes. Children with disabilities eligible under TEFRA will get full health insurance coverage under Medicaid services that include coverage with SoonerCare Child Health Program. [231]

THEORY OF MIND (TOM)
The ability to consider another person's mental state (thoughts, desires, intentions) or experience. [232, 18]

TOURETTE'S DISORDER
A medical disorder characterized by the presence of tics. A tic is an involuntary, sudden, rapid, recurrent, nonrhythmic motor movement or vocalization. Four characteristics constitute Tourette's Disorder: one or more vocal tics have been present at some time during the illness, although not necessarily concurrently; the tic(s) may wax and wane in frequency but must have persisted for more than one year since first tic onset; onset is before age eighteen; and the disturbance is not attributable to the physiological effects of a substance (e.g., cocaine) or another medical condition (e.g., Huntington's disease, post-viral encephalitis). [18]

TRANSITION
The process of bridging the time and environments between two settings, programs, or life situations. Also, moving or preparing to move from one activity to another. [4]

TRANSITION PLAN OR TRANSITION PLANNING

A part of an IEP that lays out what your teen must learn and do in high school in order to succeed as a young adult. S/he and the IEP team develop the plan together before it kicks in at age sixteen. The transition plan includes goals and activities that are academic and functional. But they extend beyond school to practical life skills and job training. [169]

TREATMENT AND EDUCATION OF AUTISTIC AND COMMUNICATION RELATED HANDICAPPED CHILDREN (TEACCH)

TEACCH is based at the University of North Carolina at Chapel Hill and is a nationally and internationally known model of conceptualizing Autism Spectrum Disorders (ASD) and delivering services and supports. It is a therapeutic approach based on ideas that autistic individuals can effectively understand visual cues as opposed to auditory cues. Picture schedules are often used to help break down tasks into manageable steps. [54, 55]

TUBEROUS SCLEROSIS

Tuberous sclerosis (TSC) is a genetic disease that causes benign tumors to grow in the brain and on other vital organs such as the kidneys, heart, eyes, lungs, and skin. It commonly affects the central nervous system. In addition to the benign tumors that frequently occur in TSC, other common symptoms include seizures, mental retardation, behavior problems, and skin abnormalities. TSC may be present at birth, but signs of the disorder can be subtle and full symptoms may take some time to develop. It occurs in 1 in 6000 births. Autism is sometimes associated with tuberous sclerosis. [4]

TWICE EXCEPTIONAL
Also referred to as "2e." A term often used to describe gifted children who have the characteristics of gifted students with high achievement potential and give evidence of one or more disabilities as defined by federal or state eligibility criteria. These disabilities may include specific learning disabilities (SLD), speech and language disorders, emotional/behavioral disorders, physical disabilities, autism spectrum, or other impairments such as attention deficit hyperactivity disorder (ADHD). [233]

VERBAL BEHAVIOR MILESTONES ASSESSMENT & PLACEMENT PROGRAM (VB-MAPP)
An assessment tool used by many early intervention and autism treatment programs to inform curriculum and programming for young children receiving Applied Behavior Analysis therapy for autism and language delays. The VB-MAPP contains three assessment areas, milestones (targeting specific language and play goals), barriers (targeting behavior challenges that inhibit progress), and transitions (evaluating the most appropriate education setting for a child). [234]

VERBAL IQ
The score resulting from various tests involving verbal tasks, such as understanding written material and answering general knowledge questions. [6]

VESTIBULAR SYSTEM
A complex set of structures and neural pathways that serves a wide variety of functions that contribute to our sense of proprioception and equilibrium. May also be referred to as our "sensory system." The functions of the vestibular system include the sensation of orientation and acceleration of the head in any

direction with associated compensation in eye movement and posture. [235]

VESTIBULAR INPUT

A sensory channel that depends on direction, position, or movement of the head. [11]

VIDEO MODELING

A therapy technique using video-based technology to teach a new behavior. Video-modeling is considered an evidence-based intervention for individuals with autism. In video-modeling, the individual watches a video or several video clips demonstrating the target behavior and then the individual performs the behavior immediately after to receives positive or corrective feedback. Video modeling can be used for many language and social skill needs. [237]

VINELAND ADAPTIVE BEHAVIOR SCALES

Considered a leading instrument for supporting the diagnosis of intellectual and developmental disabilities. The Vineland evaluates a child's daily functioning, communication, social interaction, and independence at home in the community. [236]

VISIO-SPATIAL SKILLS

These are cognitive abilities that relate to the way you perceive the objects and surroundings of your surroundings and environment. [4]

VISUAL PROCESSING

Taking visual information from the environment, accurately interpreting the visual information, and using the information to make decisions for ideas and actions. Issues of visual processing are many and varied and require a very specific diagnosis. The ability to organize visual information and use it for performance in the environment (e.g., when throwing a softball to a friend, know how far away the friend is and how hard and how far to throw the ball). Visio-spatial skills are related to the way one perceives their surroundings or objects in a certain environment. [4]

VISUAL SCHEDULE
An evidence-based intervention visual used to help children anticipate transitions and upcoming activities and understand the expected agenda for a given period (e.g., daily schedule, class period schedule). Visual schedules often consist of pictures or a combination of images and words that represent the scheduled activities in the order in which they are to be completed. [238]

VISUAL SUPPORTS
Written words, pictures and/or icons that convey information in visual medium. Individuals with autism are typically visual learners and conveying information visually assists with comprehension. [54]

WAIVERS
Prior to 1981, needed Medicaid funded services for people with intellectual disability and related disabilities were primarily available in institutional settings (e.g. nursing facilities, intermediate care facilities). People with intellectual disability and related disabilities were pushed toward institutional settings because the supportive services necessary for them to live in their own home or community setting were not available. The Home and Community-Based Services (HCBS) Waiver Program was established in 1981 and allowed states to elect to furnish under Medicaid, as an alternative to institutional care, a broad

array of services that are otherwise not covered under the Medicaid program. [239]

WECHSLER INTELLIGENCE SCALE FOR CHILDREN (WISC OR WISC-III)
An intelligence test that measures a child's intellectual ability and five cognitive domains that impact performance. It is an individually administered clinical instrument for assessing the intellectual functioning of children. [4, 240]

WECHSLER PRESCHOOL AND PRIMARY SCALE OF INTELLIGENCE—REVISED (WPPSI-R)
A clinical instrument similar to the WISC-III and the WAIS-R, except for children ages 3–0 to 7–0. [4]

WEIGHTED VEST
The concept of the weighted vest is based on the technique of deep pressure. Deep pressure is used to assist the child to self-calm and relax so that sensory stimulus can be processed. The use of a weighted vest is thought to provide the child with unconscious information from the muscles and joints. Children who are easily distracted, hyperactive, and lacking in concentration are said to respond positively to the additional weight a vest provides. [4]

THE WILBARGER PROTOCOL
Some children have a tendency to respond to certain harmless sensations as if they were dangerous or painful. This is called sensory defensiveness (SD). The child with SD may misperceive the world as dangerous, alarming or at the very least irritating. When left untreated, SD can have a negative influence on every aspect of life. The protocol uses frequent application of firm/ deep pressure touch input to various parts of the body. This is followed by gentle joint compression. [4]

WRAPAROUND
A comprehensive, holistic, youth and family-driven way of responding when children or youth experience serious mental health or behavioral challenges. Wraparound services put the child or youth and family at the center. [241]

WRAPAROUND SERVICES
Wraparound differs from many service delivery strategies in that it provides a comprehensive, holistic, youth- and family-driven way of responding when children or youth experience serious mental health or behavioral challenges. Wraparound puts the child or youth and family at the center. With support from a team of professionals and natural supports, the family's ideas and perspectives about what they need and what will be helpful drive all of the work in Wraparound. [242]

REFERENCES

1. The Understood Team. The difference between IEPs and 504 plans. in Understood for All Inc [database online]. 2022 Available from https://www.understood.org/en/articles/the-difference-between-ieps-and-504-plans (accessed September 4, 2022).

2. Dubie, Melissa, and Pratt, Cathy. Observing behavior using A-B-C data. in The Trustees of Indiana University [database online]. 2022Available from https://www.iidc.indiana.edu/irca/articles/observing-behavior-using-a-b-c-data.html (accessed September 4, 2022).

3. Smith, Leah. #ableism. in Center for Disability Rights [database online]. 2022 Available from https://cdrnys.org/blog/uncategorized/ableism.

4. Autism Community Training Society. Living & working with children with autism spectrum disorder in british columbia glossary. in ACT-Autism Community Training [database online]. 2012 Available from https://www.actcommunity.ca/files/pdf/act/manual/PM_glossary.pdf?v=2015 (accessed September 4 2022).

5. American Psychological Association. APA dictionary of psychology. in American Psychological Association [database online]. 2022 Available from https://dictionary.apa.org.

6. Autism Society of Nebraska. Glossary of terms. in Autism Society of Nebraska [database online]. 2022 Available from https://autismne-braska.org/glossary-of-terms/.

7. Verdugo Hills Autism Project. Adaptive skills. in Verdugo Hills Autism Project [database online]. 2022 Available from https://www.vhap.org/adaptive-skills/.

8. The admission, review and dismissal process. in City Scape Schools [database online]. Available from https://www.cityscapeschools.org/teaching-and-learning/special-population/the-admission-review-and-dismissal-process/.

9. Merriam-Webster.com Dictionary, s.v. "advocacy," accessed September 4, 2022, https://www.merriam-webster.com/dictionary/advocacy.

AUTISMOLOGY: An Autism Dictionary

10. One-to-one support in the classroom. in Autism New Jersey [database online]. 2022 Available from https://www.autismnj.org/article/one-on-one-support-in-the-classroom/.

11. Jeffreys, R. E. (2021). *You were made for this: Finding courage and intuition for raising a child with autism* Empowerment Publishing & Multimedia.

12. https://blogs.scientificamerican.com/mind-guest-blog/the-emotional-blindness-of-alexithymia/

13. https://www.spectroomz.com/blog/allistic-definition

14. https://www.nidcd.nih.gov/health/assistive-devices-people-hearing-voice-speech-or-language-disorders

15. https://www.ada.gov/cguide.htm#anchor62335

16. https://www.p12.nysed.gov/specialed/publications/iepguidance/annual.htm#:~:text=Annual%20goals%20are%20statements%20that,IEP%20will%20be%20in%20effect.

17. https://www.ncbi.nlm.nih.gov/pmc/articles/PMC5772195/

18. American Psychiatric Association. *Diagnostic and Statistical Manual of Mental Disorders (5ᵗʰ Ed.)* American Psychiatric Association; Washington DC, USA: 2013.

19. https://psychiatry.org/patients-families/anxiety-disorders/what-are-anxiety-disorders

20. https://www.nidcd.nih.gov/health/aphasia

21. https://www.bacb.com/about-behavior-analysis/

22. https://www.ninds.nih.gov/Disorders/All-Disorders/Apraxia-Information-Page

23. https://childdevelopment.com.au/areas-of-concern/talking/articulation-pronunciation-and-talking/

24. https://www.aane.org/glossary/

25. https://www.autismspeaks.org/types-autism-what-asperger-syndrome

26. https://www.nidcd.nih.gov/health/
assistive-devices-people-hearing-voice-speech-or-language-disorders

27. https://www.washington.edu/doit/what-assistive-technology

28. https://medical-dictionary.thefreedictionary.com/atypical

29. https://www.asha.org/policy/sp2018-00353/

30. http://auditoryintegrationtraining.co.uk/auditory-integration-train-
ing-ait-for-hearing-autism-adhd-add-dyslexia-and-other-special-needs-2/
auditory-integration-training-ait-for-hearing-autism-adhd-add-dyslexia-
and-other-special-needs/

31. https://www.nhs.uk/conditions/auditory-processing-disorder/

32. https://www.health.ny.gov/community/infants_children/early_inter-
vention/disorders/autism/screenin.htm

33. https://www.sciencedirect.com/topics/medicine-and-dentistry/
autism-diagnostic-observation-schedule

34. http://autismmentalstatusexam.com/

35. https://www.autism.org.uk/about/what-is/asd.aspx

36. https://www.verywellhealth.com/what-is-an-autistic-savant-260033#:

37. Patten, E., Belardi, K., Baranek, G. T., Watson, L. R., Labban, J. D., &
Oller, D. K. (2014). Vocal patterns in infants with autism spectrum
disorder: canonical babbling status and vocalization frequency.
Journal of autism and developmental disorders, 44(10), 2413–2428.
https://doi.org/10.1007/s10803-014-2047-4

38. Merriam-Webster. (n.d.). Baseline. In Merriam-Webster.com
dictionary. Retrieved from https://www.merriam-webster.com/
dictionary/baseline

39. Ballot, D. E., Ramdin, T., Rakotsoane, D., Agaba, F., Davies, V. A.,
Chirwa, T., & Cooper, P. A. (2017). Use of the Bayley Scales of Infant

and Toddler Development, Third Edition, to Assess Developmental Outcome in Infants and Young Children in an Urban Setting in South Africa. International scholarly research notices, 2017, 1631760. https://doi.org/10.1155/2017/1631760

40. https://www.understood.org/en/learning-thinking-differences/treatments-approaches/educational-strategies/behavior-intervention-plans-what-you-need-to-know

41. https://members.ccbh.com/health-topics/resources/behavioral-health-rehabilitation-services-bhrs

42. Lee, Ember & Stahmer, Aubyn & Reed, S. & Searcy, Karyn & Brookman-Frazee, Lauren. (2011). *Differential Learning of a Blended Intervention Approach Among Therapists of Varied Backgrounds.*

43. https://www.health.ny.gov/community/infants_children/early_intervention/disorders/autism/screenin.htm

44. https://www.apa.org/depression-guideline/child-behavior-checklist.pdf

45. Merriam-Webster. (n.d.). Cognitive. In Merriam-Webster.com dictionary. Retrieved from https://www.merriam-webster.com/dictionary/cognitive

46. https://www.apa.org/ptsd-guideline/patients-and-families/cognitive-behavioral

47. https://www1.health.gov.au/internet/publications/publishing.nsf/Content/drugtreat-pubs-comorbid-toc~drugtreat-pubs-comorbid-4~drugtreat-pubs-comorbid-4-3

48. Merriam-Webster. (n.d.). Convulsion. In Merriam-Webster.com dictionary. Retrieved from https://www.merriam-webster.com/dictionary/convulsion

49. https://medical-dictionary.thefreedictionary.com/coping+skill

50. https://www.complextrauma.org/glossary/co-regulation/

51. https://my.clevelandclinic.org/health/articles/22187-cortisol

52. Merriam-Webster. (n.d.). Cue. In Merriam-Webster.com dictionary. Retrieved from https://www.merriam-webster.com/dictionary/cue

53. http://www.med.umich.edu/yourchild/topics/devdel.htm

54. https://www.easterseals.com/explore-resources/living-with-autism/glossary-of-autism-disorders.html

55. Shea V. (2013) Treatment and Education of Autistic and Related Communication-Handicapped Children. In: Volkmar F.R. (eds) Encyclopedia of Autism Spectrum Disorders. Springer, New York, NY. https://doi.org/10.1007/978-1-4419-1698-3_949

56. https://www.cdc.gov/ncbddd/developmentaldisabilities/facts.html#ref

57. https://www.cdc.gov/ncbddd/wicguide/developmentalmonitoring.html

58. https://www.autismspeaks.org/expert-opinion/what-discrete-trial-training

59. https://www.webmd.com/mental-health/what-is-dopamine

60. https://www.cdc.gov/ncbddd/birthdefects/downsyndrome.html

61. https://www.advocacyinstitute.org/resources/Preparing.for.SpEd.Mediation.Resolution.Sessions.pdf

62. https://www.dictionary.com/browse/dx

63. https://dibels.uoregon.edu/assessment/dibels

64. https://www.understood.org/en/learning-thinking-differences/child-learning-disabilities/dyspraxia/understanding-dyspraxia

65. https://www.cdc.gov/ncbddd/actearly/parents/states.html

66. https://www.medicaid.gov/medicaid/benefits/early-and-periodic-screening-diagnostic-and-treatment/index.html

67. https://www.autism.org.uk/about/communication/communicating.aspx

68. https://www.ehlers-danlos.com/what-is-eds/

69. https://www.hopkinsmedicine.org/health/treatment-tests-and-therapies/electroencephalogram-eeg

70. https://www.sunnydays.com/glossary

71. https://www.marcus.org/autism-resources/autism-tips-and-resources/what-to-do-when-your-child-elopes

72. http://www.selfinjury.bctr.cornell.edu/perch/resources/what-is-emotion-regulationsinfo-brief.pdf

73. https://www.mayoclinic.org/diseases-conditions/epilepsy/symptoms-causes/syc-20350093

74. https://www.goodtherapy.org/learn-about-therapy/types/equine-assisted-therapy

75. https://www.apa.org/topics/psychological-testing-assessment

76. https://www.aane.org/glossary/

77. https://audiology-speech.com/expressive-language/

78. https://cdn5-ss2.sharpschool.com/UserFiles/Servers/Server_3265386/File/Student%20Services/Extended%20School%20Year/Services%20Beyond%20the%20School%20Year.pdf

79. Cañigueral, R., & Hamilton, A. (2019). The Role of Eye Gaze During Natural Social Interactions in Typical and Autistic People. *Frontiers in psychology*, 10, 560. https://doi.org/10.3389/fpsyg.2019.00560

80. https://www.faceblind.org/research/

81. https://chicagoabatherapy.com/articles/peditric-aba-therapy-terms-e-k/

82. https://www.understood.org/en/learning-thinking-differences/
child-learning-disabilities/movement-coordination-issues/
all-about-fine-motor-skills

83. https://asatonline.org/research-treatment/clinical-corner/
food-selectivity/

84. https://ghr.nlm.nih.gov/condition/
fragile-x-syndrome#sourcesforpage

85. https://www.understood.org/en/school-learning/your-childs-rights/
basics-about-childs-rights/what-is-and-isnt-covered-under-fape

86. https://connectability.ca/2011/06/13/
supporting-children-with-asd-module-6/

87. https://www.understood.org/en/articles/
functional-assessment-what-it-is-and-how-it-works

88. https://www.ncbi.nlm.nih.gov/pmc/articles/PMC2846575/

89. https://www.ifm.org/functional-medicine/
what-is-functional-medicine/

90. https://connectability.ca/2011/06/13/
supporting-children-with-asd-module-6/

91. de Marchena, A. B., Eigsti, I. M., & Yerys, B. E. (2015). Brief
report: generalization weaknesses in verbally fluent children and
adolescents with autism spectrum disorder. *Journal of autism and
developmental disorders*, 45(10), 3370–3376. https://doi.org/10.1007/
s10803-015-2478-6

92. https://socialsci.libretexts.org/Bookshelves/Sociology/Book%3A_
Sociology_(Boundless)/03%3A_Culture/3.02%3A_The_Symbolic_
Nature_of_Culture/3.2F%3A_Gestures

93. Karren, B. C. (2017). A Test Review: Gilliam, JE (2014). Gilliam
Autism Rating Scale–Third Edition (GARS-3).

94. https://www.lifehack.org/863723/what-are-goals

95. https://www.stanleygreenspan.com/resources/research

96. https://www.understood.org/en/learning-thinking-differences/child-learning-disabilities/movement-coordination-issues/all-about-gross-motor-skills

97. https://www.dictionary.com/browse/group-home

98. https://legaldictionary.net/guardianship/

99. https://www.legalzoom.com/articles/healthcare-power-of-attorney

100. https://www.cdc.gov/phlp/publications/topic/hipaa.html

101. https://www.dignityhealth.org/articles/what-is-holistic-health-care-anyway#:~:text=Holistic%20health%20is%20about%20caring,Take%20stress%2C%20for%20example.

102. https://www.c-q-l.org/resources/guides/hcbs-guide-your-right-to-a-community-life/

103. https://chatwithus.org/conditions/hyperlexia/

104. Schultz-Krohn W. (2013) Hyperresponsiveness. In: Volkmar F.R. (eds) *Encyclopedia of Autism Spectrum Disorders*. Springer, New York, NY

105. https://www.physio.co.uk/what-we-treat/paediatric/problems/neurological-problems/abnormal-muscle-tone/hypertonia.php

106. Schultz-Krohn W. (2013) Hyporesponsiveness. In: Volkmar F.R. (eds) *Encyclopedia of Autism Spectrum Disorders*. Springer, New York, NY

107. https://my.clevelandclinic.org/health/diseases/21156-low-blood-pressure-hypotension#:~:text=Hypotension%2C%20also%20known%20as%20low,including%20dizziness%2C%20fainting%20and%20more.

108. https://www.nhs.uk/conditions/hypotonia/

109. https://www.massadvocates.org/news/ask-a-self-advocate-the-pros-and-cons-of-person-first-and-identity-first-language#:~:text=Identity%2Dfirst%20language%20is%20language,as%20being%20a%20disabled%20person.

110. Thomas B. (2013) Idiosyncratic Language. In: Volkmar F.R. (eds) *Encyclopedia of Autism Spectrum Disorders.* Springer, New York, NY

111. https://researchautism.org/the-importance-of-peers-in-inclusive-education-for-individuals-with-asd/

112. https://www.inclusion.me.uk/news/what_does_inclusion_mean

113. https://www.verywellfamily.com/independent-educational-evaluation-3106871

114. https://www.disabilityrightsca.org/publications/how-to-obtain-an-independent-educational-evaluation-at-public-expense

115. https://www.disabilityrightsca.org/publications/the-individualized-plan-for-employment-ipe-fact-sheet

116. https://www.understood.org/en/school-learning/special-services/504-plan/the-difference-between-ieps-and-504-plans

117. https://www.understood.org/en/learning-thinking-differences/treatments-approaches/early-intervention/ifsp-what-it-is-and-how-it-works

118. Wehman P., Carr S. (2013) Individualized Transition Plan (ITP). In: Volkmar F.R. (eds) *Encyclopedia of Autism Spectrum Disorders.* Springer, New York, NY. https://doi.org/10.1007/978-1-4419-1698-3_1798

119. https://www.apa.org/advocacy/education/idea

120. https://www.verywellmind.com/what-is-the-average-iq-2795284

121. Xyrichis A, Lowton K. What fosters or prevents interprofessional teamworking in primary or community care? A literature review. *J Nurs Stud.* 2008;45:140–143. doi: 10.1016/j.ijnurstu.2007.01.015.

122. https://www.who.int/classifications/icd/en/

123. https://www.med.unc.edu/ahs/asap/resources/about-joint-attention/

124. https://psychcentral.com/disorders/language-disorder/

125. https://www.understood.org/en/school-learning/
special-services/special-education-basics/
least-restrictive-environment-lre-what-you-need-to-know

126. https://serr.disabilityrightsca.org/serr-manual/chapter-1-informa-
tion-on-basic-rights/1-52-what-does-least-restrictive-environment-
lre-mean/

127. Farmer C. (2013) Leiter International Performance Scale-Re-
vised (Leiter-R). In: Volkmar F.R. (eds) *Encyclopedia of Autism
Spectrum Disorders*. Springer, New York, NY. https://doi.
org/10.1007/978-1-4419-1698-3_1643

128. https://www.verywellhealth.com/
what-are-the-three-levels-of-autism-260233

129. https://www.law.cornell.edu/cfr/text/34/303.23

130. https://www.understood.org/en/school-learning/
special-services/special-education-basics/
least-restrictive-environment-lre-what-you-need-to-know

131. https://www.mayoclinic.org/diseases-conditions/depression/
symptoms-causes/syc-20356007

132. https://www.healthline.com/health/autism/
autism-masking#definition

133. https://www.advocacyinstitute.org/resources/Preparing.for.SpEd.
Mediation.Resolution.Sessions.pdf

134. https://www.medicaid.gov/medicaid/index.html

135. https://www.autism.org.uk/about/behaviour/meltdowns.aspx

136. https://dictionary.cambridge.org/us/dictionary/english/
metacognitive

137. https://www.mindful.org/meditation/mindfulness-getting-started/

138. https://positivepsychology.com/mobile-therapy/

139. https://m-chat.org

140. https://www.health.harvard.edu/blog/what-is-neurodiversity-202111232645

141. https://www.disabled-world.com/disability/awareness/neurodiversity/

142. http://fpddev.com/staging/aane2/glossary/neurodiversity/

143. *Sean Inderbitzen verbally quoted this to me

144. *Sean Inderbitzen verbally quoted this to me

145. https://www.urmc.rochester.edu/highland/departments-centers/neurology/what-is-a-neurologist.aspx

146. https://braintherapytms.com/neuroplasticity-and-autism/

147. https://www.aane.org/glossary/

148. https://www.k12.wa.us/policy-funding/grants-grant-management/every-student-succeeds-act-essa-implemen-tation/elementary-and-secondary-education-act-esea/no-child-left-behind-act-2001

149. Dunn D. (2013) Notice of Recommended Educational Placement (NOREP). In: Volkmar F.R. (eds) *Encyclopedia of Autism Spectrum Disorders*. Springer, New York, NY. https://doi.org/10.1007/978-1-4419-1698-3_389

150. https://www.aota.org/Conference-Events/OTMonth/what-is-OT.aspx

151. https://www2.ed.gov/about/offices/list/ocr/aboutocr.html

152. https://www.justice.gov/archives/olp/alternative-dispute-resolution

153. Bean A. (2013) Oral-Motor Skills. In: Volkmar F.R. (eds) *Encyclopedia of Autism Spectrum Disorders*. Springer, New York, NY. https://doi.org/10.1007/978-1-4419-1698-3_1685

154. http://www.projectidealonline.org/v/orthopedic-impairments/

155. https://www.simplypsychology.org/parasympathetic-nervous-system.html

156. https://www.autism.org.uk/advice-and-guidance/topics/diagnosis/pda/parents-and-carers

157. https://www.autism.org.uk/advice-and-guidance/topics/diagnosis/pda

158. https://rarediseases.info.nih.gov/diseases/7312/pediatric-autoim-mune-neuropsychiatric-disorders-associated-with-streptococcus-infec-tions

159. https://www.ncbi.nlm.nih.gov/pmc/articles/PMC5087797/#:~:tex-t=Peer%20mediated%20intervention%20(PMI)%20is,initiations%2C%20responses%2C%20and%20interactions.

160. https://www.understood.org/en/articles/persevera-tion-adhd-and-learning-differences#:~:text=Perseveration%20is%20when%20someone%20%E2%80%9Cgets,actions%2C%20and%20thoughts%2C%20too.

161. https://www.ninds.nih.gov/health-information/disorders/pervasive-developmental-disorders#:~:tex-t=Publications-,Definition,before%203%20years%20of%20age.

162. Merriam-Webster. (n.d.). Physical therapy. In Merriam-Webster.com dictionary. Retrieved August 12, 2020, from https://www.merri-am-webster.com/dictionary/physical%20therapy

163. https://www.nationalautismresources.com/the-picture-exchange-communication-system-pecs/

164. https://education.ucsb.edu/autism/pivotal-response-treatment

165. https://www.ncbi.nlm.nih.gov/pmc/articles/PMC3108032/

166. https://www.mayoclinic.org/diseases-conditions/prader-willi-syndrome/symptoms-causes/syc-20355997

167. Lam Y.G. (2014) Pragmatic Language in Autism: An Overview. In: Patel V., Preedy V., Martin C. (eds) *Comprehensive Guide to Autism.* Springer, New York, NY + DSM V pg 824

168. https://www.autism.org.uk/about/behaviour/obsessions-repetitive-routines.aspx

169. https://nationalautismassociation.org/store/#!/ASD-&-the-IEP-Process-Toolkit/p/113968033/category=23350149

170. https://www.parentcompanion.org/article/present-levels-of-academic-achievement-and-functional-performance-plaafp#:~:text=The%20Present%20Levels%20of%20Academic,his%20initial%20special%20education%20evaluation.

171. https://www.apraxia-kids.org/apraxia_kids_library/prosody-and-articulation/

172. Gabig C.S. (2013) Protodeclarative. In: Volkmar F.R. (eds) *Encyclopedia of Autism Spectrum Disorders.* Springer, New York, NY

173. Goodhart, F., & Baron-Cohen, S. (1993). How many ways can the point be made? Evidence from children with and without autism. First Language, 13(38), 225–233. https://doi.org/10.1177/014272379301303804

174. Dunn D. (2013) Public Law 94-142. In: Volkmar F.R. (eds) Encyclopedia of Autism Spectrum Disorders. Springer, New York, NY. https://doi.org/10.1007/978-1-4419-1698-3_393

175. https://www.afasic.org.uk/about-talking/more-about-speech-language-and-communication/

176. https://www.theravive.com/therapedia/language-disorder-dsm–5-315.39-(f80.9)

177. Merriam-Webster. (n.d.). Regression. In Merriam-Webster.com dictionary. Retrieved August 12, 2020, from https://www.merriam-webster.com/dictionary/regression

178. https://dictionary.apa.org/reinforcement

179. https://www.understood.org/en/school-learning/special-services/ special-education-basics/related-services-for-kids-with-learning-and-thinking-differences-what-you-need-to-know

180. https://www.autismspeaks.org/ relationship-development-intervention-rdi-0

181. https://www.autism.org.uk/about/behaviour/obsessions-repeti-tive-routines.aspx

182. https://www.ssa.gov/payee/faqrep.htm?tl=5

183. https://www.nia.nih.gov/health/what-respite-care

184. https://www.understood.org/en/school-learning/special-services/ rti/understanding-response-to-intervention

185. https://www.theedadvocate.org/edupedia/content/ what-is-reverse-mainstreaming/

186. Hsu, W. S., & Ho, M. H. (2009). Ritual behaviours of children with autism spectrum disorders in Taiwan. *Journal of intellectual & developmental disability*, 34(4), 290–295. https://doi.org/10.3109/13668250903291901

187. https://scautism.org/get-started/aba-therapy/

188. https://www.cdc.gov/ncbddd/autism/screening.html

189. https://www.hopkinsmedicine.org/health/conditions-and-diseases/ epilepsy/types-of-seizures

190. Pretzel R.E., Hester A.D., Porr S. (2013) Self-help Skills. In: Volkmar F.R. (eds) *Encyclopedia of Autism Spectrum Disorders*. Springer, New York, NY. https://doi.org/10.1007/978-1-4419-1698-3_943

191. https://www.autism.org.uk/about/behaviour/challenging-behaviour/ self-injury.aspx

192. https://asdonthego.ku.edu/self-monitoring-0

193. https://www.autism.org.uk/about/behaviour/obsessions-repetitive-routines.aspx

194. Kapp, S. K., Steward, R., Crane, L., Elliott, D., Elphick, C., Pellicano, E., & Russell, G. (2019). 'People should be allowed to do what they like': Autistic adults' views and experiences of stimming. *Autism: the international journal of research and practice*, 23 (7), 1782–1792. https://doi.org/10.1177/1362361319829628

195. https://www.understood.org/en/learning-thinking-differences/treatments-approaches/therapies/sensory-diet-treatment-what-you-need-to-know

196. https://www.understood.org/en/learning-thinking-differences/child-learning-disabilities/sensory-processing-issues/sensory-seeking-and-sensory-avoiding-what-you-need-to-know

197. https://www.healthychildren.org/English/health-issues/conditions/developmental-disabilities/Pages/Sensory-Integration-Therapy.aspx

198. https://sensorimotorpsychotherapy.org/about/#what-is-sp

199. https://www.webmd.com/children/sensory-processing-disorder#1

200. https://www.autism.org.uk/about/behaviour/sensory-world.aspx##senses

201. https://www.findresources.co.uk/the-syndromes/cri-du-chat/sensory-stimulation-sensory-reinforcement

202. https://www.autismspeaks.org/assistance-dog-information

203. https://www.carautismroadmap.org/the-role-of-the-service-coordinator/

204. https://www.asha.org/public/speech/development/social-communication/

205. https://casel.org/fundamentals-of-sel/

206. https://kathysmusic.com/using-imitative-play-to-boost-your/

207. https://open.lib.umn.edu/sociology/
chapter/5-3-social-interaction-in-everyday-life/

208. https://www.asha.org/PRPSpecificTopic.
aspx?folderid=8589935303&section=Signs_and_Symptoms

209. https://childdevelopment.com.au/areas-of-concern/
play-and-social-skills/social-skills/

210. Jordan, C. J., & Caldwell-Harris, C. L. (2012). Understanding differences in neurotypical and autism spectrum special interests through
Internet forums. *Intellectual and developmental disabilities*, 50(5),
391–402. https://doi.org/10.1352/1934-9556-50.5.391

211. https://www.autismspeaks.org/autism-school-your-childs-rights

212. https://www.specialneedsalliance.org/the-voice/
your-special-needs-trust-snt-defined-2/

213. https://www.specialolympics.org/about

214. https://sites.ed.gov/idea/regs/b/a/300.39

215. Merriam-Webster. (n.d.). Speech therapy. In Merriam-Webster.com
dictionary. Retrieved August 12, 2020, from https://www.merri-
am-webster.com/dictionary/speech%20therapy

216. https://www.asha.org/Students/Speech-Language-Pathology/

217. https://www.agnesian.com/blog/application-savant-and-splin-
ter-skills-autistic-population-through-educational-curriculum

218. https://autismwestmidlands.org.uk/wp-content/uploads/2020/10/
Spoon-Theory.pdf

219. https://www.theravive.com/therapedia/
stereotypic-movement-disorder-dsm–5-307.3-(f98.4)

220. https://www.mayoclinic.org/diseases-conditions/mental-illness/
in-depth/mental-health/art-20046477

221. https://www.ssa.gov/benefits/ssi/

222. https://supporteddecisions.org/about-supported-decision-making/

223. https://ddrcco.com/accessing-services/supported-living

224. https://babysparks.com/2017/04/28/
symbolic-play-imagination-comes-to-life/

225. https://www.medicinenet.com/sympathetic_nervous_system/
definition.htm

226. https://www.autism.org.uk/about/behaviour/sensory-world.
aspx##senses

227. Merriam-Webster. (n.d.). Syndrome. In Merriam-Webster.com
dictionary. Retrieved August 12, 2020, from https://www.merriam-
webster.com/dictionary/syndrome

228. https://www.stanfordchildrens.org/en/topic/
default?id=temper-tantrums-90-P02295

229. https://www.usability.gov/how-to-and-tools/methods/task-analysis.
html

230. https://ciswh.org/wp-content/uploads/2016/02/TEFRA-policy-brief.
pdf

231. https://www.okabletech.org/resources/at-funding-guide/
edicaid-tefra

232. Shea V. (2013) Treatment and Education of Autistic and Related
Communication-Handicapped Children. In: Volkmar F.R. (eds)
Encyclopedia of Autism Spectrum Disorders. Springer, New York, NY.
https://doi.org/10.1007/978-1-4419-1698-3_949

233. https://www.nagc.org/resources-publications/resources-parents/
twice-exceptional-students

234. https://chicagoabatherapy.com/articles/
what-is-the-vb-mapp-how-is-it-used-in-pediatric-aba-therapy/

235. Casale J, Browne T, Murray I, et al. Physiology, Vestibular System.
[Updated 2020 May 24]. In: StatPearls [Internet]. Treasure Island

(FL): StatPearls Publishing; 2020 Jan-. Available from: https://www.ncbi.nlm.nih.gov/books/NBK532978/

236. https://www.pearsonassessments.com/store/usassessments/en/Store/Professional-Assessments/Behavior/Adaptive/Vineland-Adaptive-Behavior-Scales-%7C-Third-Edition/p/100001622.html

237. https://raisingchildren.net.au/autism/therapies-guide/video-modelling

238. Ray-Subramanian C. (2013) Visual Schedule. In: Volkmar F.R. (eds) *Encyclopedia of Autism Spectrum Disorders*. Springer, New York, N

239. https://ddsn.sc.gov/services/medicaid-home-and-community-based-waiver-services

240. https://www.pearsonassessments.com/store/usassessments/en/Store/Professional-Assessments/Cognition-%26-Neuro/Gifted-%26-Talented/Wechsler-Intelligence-Scale-for-Children-%7C-Fifth-Edition-/p/100000771.html

241. https://nwi.pdx.edu/wraparound-basics/#whatisWraparound

242. https://nwi.pdx.edu/wraparound-basics/

243. https://raisingchildren.net.au/autism/behaviour/common-concerns/stimming-asd

ABOUT THE AUTHOR

 Tosha Rollins is a Licensed Professional Counselor in South Carolina and the owner of Rollins Counseling, LLC. She is wife to Travis and momma to three sons—Jason, Jacob, and Konnor, ages 9 to 23—and stepmom to Kaylee, who is now in college. She has two sons on the autism spectrum. She loves adventures, traveling, nature, and spending time with her family. Tosha also enjoys serving the community as a Lead with Love Safety Plan Coordinator. Tosha is an autism advocate, public speaker, published author, and podcaster. In 2018 she started the *Autism in Action* podcast to help families connect with autism resources, services, and support. When she is not working, she is spending quality time with her family and planning her next adventure.

Continue your quest for knowledge
with these perennial favorites

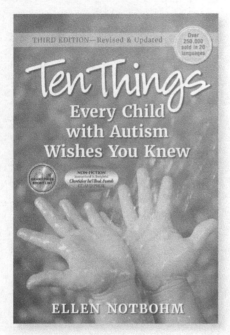